Praise for

52 Weeks to Fortify Your Family

"*52 Weeks* is an awesome resource for introducing a topical study of the scriptures to your family routine. And since you don't have to come up with the topics and verses yourself, you can spend more time actually discussing the scriptures as a family. I love that there are conference talks included as well! Consistent gospel habits have made all the difference in my family, and that's exactly what this book will help you to create."

—Heidi Doxey, author of the Tiny Talks series

"Bring scripture power and daily devotionals on courage, faith, forgiveness, and much more into your home with Carpenter's inspired compilation, which is destined to fortify and uplift you and your family year-round."

— Annalisa Hall, author of *I Want to Be Baptized* and *The Holy Ghost Is like a Blanket*

NICOLE CARPENTER

CFI
An Imprint of Cedar Fort, Inc.
Springville, Utah

No part of this book may be reproduced in any form whatsoever, whether by graphic, visual, electronic, film, microfilm, tape recording, or any other means, without prior written permission of the publisher, except in the case of brief passages embodied in critical reviews and articles.

This is not an official publication of The Church of Jesus Christ of Latter-day Saints. The opinions and views expressed herein belong solely to the author and do not necessarily represent the opinions or views of Cedar Fort, Inc. Permission for the use of sources, graphics, and photos is also solely the responsibility of the author.

ISBN 13: 978-1-4621-1606-5

Published by CFI, an imprint of Cedar Fort, Inc.
2373 W. 700 S., Springville, UT 84663
Distributed by Cedar Fort, Inc., www.cedarfort.com

LIBRARY OF CONGRESS CATALOGING-IN-PUBLICATION DATA

Carpenter, Nicole, 1980- author.
52 weeks to fortify your family / Nicole Carpenter.
    pages cm
Summary: Fifty-two devotionals to help parents fortify their children with the word of God before they send them out the door in the morning or to their beds at night.
ISBN 978-1-4621-1606-5 (alk. paper)
1. Christian life--Mormon authors. 2. Church of Jesus Christ of Latter-day Saints--Doctrines. 3. Mormon Church--Doctrines. I. Title. II. Title: Fifty-two weeks to fortify your family.

BX8656.C36 2015
249--dc23

                           2014039450

Cover design by Shawnda T. Craig
Cover design © 2015 Lyle Mortimer
Edited and typeset by Kevin Haws

Printed in the United States of America

10 9 8 7 6 5 4 3 2 1

Printed on acid-free paper

Contents

Contents

Acknowledgments

I would like to graciously thank the following:

Marty, my eternal husband and dearest friend. Words cannot express just how much I love you and how special you are to me. Thank you for your unconditional love and continuous support in all I do, even through all my crazy, ambitious ideas. Thank you for your faithful example and dedicated efforts to fortify our family.

My beautiful children, Katelyn, Cameron, Davis, and Mason, who fill my life with such joy and wonder. You make me a better person, and I am honored to be your mother. I have a secret for you: *I love you!*

Each faithful parent who wanted to strengthen their children with the scriptures and downloaded or shared the original "Armor Your Children Devotional Series" on *MOMentity.com*. You don't know it, but your thoughtful emails and encouraging comments fortified me as I refined those simple devotionals into this book.

Emily Chambers and the great team at Cedar Fort. Emily, thank you for seeing the potential in my manuscript and diligently following up with me. To think this book could have never happened all because of a spam folder.

And, most importantly, my Heavenly Father. Thank You for blessing me with the privilege of bringing to pass such an incredible tool for families everywhere. Thank You for being patient with me when I didn't listen to Your promptings the first (or fifteenth) time. And thank You for trusting me to share Your message with the world.

Preface

I admit it. Several times I have selfishly coerced my children into promising me they'll stay little forever. They never keep their promise. They keep growing up. I guess I'm okay with it—after all, that's what kids do. Yet during one particular month in 2012, my children getting bigger seemed extra heavy on my heart.

It was the end of summer and school was just around the corner. My oldest, Katelyn, was about to start second grade. Strangely, I was having a hard time with this transition. She had been in school all day long for an entire year now, but something about that moment pulled at me. Was she turning eight soon?

In just a couple months, she would be baptized a member of the Church, and I knew that for the first time in her sweet life, Satan would be there tempting her. That thought really bothered me.

Her entire life I'd wanted to protect her. I was already worried about conversations on the playground and bullies in the lunchroom. And now I wanted so badly to protect her from Satan too. I knew our home was a safe haven, but what would happen when I sent her out the door each morning? I wanted to cover her in bubble wrap and keep her body, mind, and spirit safe. Obviously that would be impossible, or at least impractical. But I realized I could (and should) do a better job of spiritually preparing her each morning before she left our home. I could armor her with the word of God.

I decided we could study a topic each week, one scripture each morning. It would be quick and easy and hopefully effective.

My mother always called the shower her "think-tank." When I'd ask her for advice, she'd say, "Let me shower on it." Maybe it's a learned behavior or a gift passed down from her, but the shower is now my think-tank too, and I'm so thankful for it.

My best ideas and most powerful inspiration usually come from within the steam of my shower. Often I'll use my index finger to fill the glass pane with words and ideas as quickly as I can before the fog takes them away, hoping that will help me remember them long enough to dry off and grab a notebook (which I keep close by).

It was there that Heavenly Father prompted me to start creating these morning devotionals for my daughter and for other families too. I felt I should make them a bigger deal and post them to my *MOMentity.com* blog for others to download for free. Having been a blogger since 2007, I knew just how much work this would be. So I ignored the prompting. But as I showered every day, the promptings came again. Reluctantly, I listened and took action. I decided I'd call the continual blog posts the "Armor Your Children Devotional Series." And with the start of school quickly approaching, I had to work fast.

I sat at my desk, staring at what should have been my website. I should have seen my yellow and pink logo across the masthead. Instead, I saw a black web page, an Iranian flag, and a message from Internet hackers informing me my website had been taken over. I took a screen shot as evidence but still could not believe my eyes.

Just four hours earlier, I had posted the very first edition of "Armor Your Children." It included a free download for anyone to print. I also wrote, "I believe in God. I believe in families. And I believe it is our responsibility to strengthen our children."

Could this have anything to do with the hackers? *MOMentity.com*, at the time, was a newer website with little traffic. To this day, I don't know for sure why it was picked from millions of others. But I believe it had everything to do with my Christian blog post.

The website was down for several hours until my website guru, James, and I could get back in and increase the site security. We've never been hacked since.

I have a love-hate relationship with Pinterest. While I love the pretty images, the useful life hacks, the picture-perfect recipes, and the birthday party ideas, I hate how the beautiful images make life seem so unrealistically perfect and the recipes haunt me because I never cook them. Most of the things on Pinterest remind so many of us of our weaknesses, not our strengths.

However, when it came to "Armor Your Children," I loved Pinterest. Because of the site, the devotional series spread like wildfire and families all over the world found the spiritual help they were looking for to fortify their families.

Comments and emails began to pour in:

"Thank you so much for sharing this! I've wanted to start reading the scriptures with my kids at breakfast, and this is perfect!!"

"I was just trying to organize something like this in my mind. Thank you for sharing!"

"I actually cried when I saw this because it was just what I needed."

"God is amazing! Just yesterday in Sunday School we were talking about developing routines that include spiritual conversations with your children in the morning, when driving, while eating, and at bedtime. Mornings are a struggle for me and I asked [for help] in this area and here it is!"

"We have been doing these devotionals every morning and my kids have all told me how much better their days are at school because of it! Thanks!"

And with each email, I would sit back, immersed in gratitude, and thank Heavenly Father for the privilege of serving Him—and then go to work creating more. Soon, over thirty weeks of scripture devotionals were available online.

Most moms with small children dream of a day alone in a hotel room with room service available at the push of a button. In the daydream, the room is so quiet you can hear yourself think, with no one screaming forty variations of "mommy" every hour.

One weekend in late April 2014, this dream became my reality. I joined my husband on a trip to Jackson Hole, Wyoming. While he was off in meetings all day long, I tucked myself away with room service, a plush hotel robe, and my laptop. I had one goal: submit a manuscript to publishers.

Ever since I was a little girl, I've always wanted to be a nonfiction author. I think this makes me strange, or maybe *unique* is a nicer term. Most people I meet like books about vampires, murder mysteries, or historical romance. Though I love a magical world of wizards, my nightstand is full of self-help and inspirational books—most of them never finished, all of them started.

My first book idea never left my computer, and rightfully so. It wasn't that good of an idea. My second book idea actually had potential, and I submitted manuscripts around to different publishers and got rejection notifications from all of those publishers. No matter how strong you think you are, rejection letters sting a bit.

Yet we have dreams for a reason. Our dreams are part of who we are, part of who we are meant to become, and part of the mission we are here to accomplish.

While in my think-tank one spring morning, I wondered about taking the "Armor Your Children" series to the masses through a book. The thought of submitting it to a publisher didn't leave my mind for the next twelve months. But rejection hurts and my ego was in the way. And it would take an entire year for me to get up the courage—in that Jackson Hole hotel room—to reach out to publishers again.

My hope is that every home will have a tattered and worn copy of this book. Not because I want to sell lots of copies (though that would be cool), but because I believe there is power in the scripture themes within. I believe in the power of these daily devotionals because *you* have told me so. Well, maybe not you exactly, but someone like you: a Christian parent seeking a way to strengthen their children and prepare them for the day, giving them strength to withstand this world.

I know there has been opposition all along the way during this process, from an idea in my bathroom to a spot on your bookshelf. So I can pretty much guarantee you will face some opposition too when you try and share these daily scriptures with your family. Please don't quit. Please keep trying. It only takes a few minutes a day, and I know you can find just a few minutes each day. You've got this!

As I search the scriptures section by section and theme by theme, I realize how simple our Heavenly Father has made His gospel and His plan of happiness. There is a clear path for us to follow. If we can remain strong and overcome the natural man, we can find the joy the Holy Ghost can bring into our lives.

I am so grateful for the Prophet Joseph Smith and his great sacrifices in bringing about the Book of Mormon, the Doctrine and Covenants, and the Pearl of Great Price. I'm so grateful for the clarifications these additional scriptures bring. How blessed we are to know the full gospel of Jesus Christ.

I'm incredibly grateful for Jesus Christ and His dedication to His mission here on earth. He faithfully served the Father and in doing so provided the only way for us to return to Him.

I have come to realize that each of these topics we will study in this book points back to one thing: the plan of salvation and the joy our Father wants to bestow on us. Honesty, obedience, courage, service, peace, talents, judgment, riches—it doesn't matter what topic. It all comes back to our Father's love for us, our Savior's love for us, and the plan of salvation that seals it all together. It's all about love.

Let's Begin!

We are raising our children in a volatile world. The lines between right and wrong and good and evil continue to fade. We worry about our children and pray that they are strong enough to handle it all.

They totally are. But we can fortify them even more.

As parents, we have the opportunity—the obligation—to teach our "children light and truth, according to the commandments" (D&C 93:42). Together, we can use the scriptures in our homes to offer our children "the whole armour of God, that [they] may be able to withstand in the evil day" (Ephesians 6:13).

52 Weeks to Fortify Your Family: 5-Minute Messages is your chest plate and helmet and sword. These five-minute messages will strengthen you and your children and give them light in a darkening world.

There is no wrong way of approaching the chapters ahead of you. As you turn to the scriptures, this can be your guidebook to spiritually strengthen your family, one simple topic at a time. Each day you can share a poignant message with your family in under five minutes. I promise that those five minutes will be some of the most important minutes you spend with your family all day, every day.

The following 52 weeks (or chapters) are divided into four overarching sections: value lessons, life lessons, gospel lessons, and holiday lessons. You can flip this page and begin right away with the first value lesson or you can search the contents page each week and pick a topic that suits your family's needs.

You'll notice on the contents page that each chapter has a check box so you can mark each topic off when you have completed it. This is to help you jump around and between the lessons and remember what you have covered. I actually encourage you to jump around. Use the holiday lessons at the back of the book during the appropriate time of year, or prayerfully pick a topic each week that will resonate with your children.

Each chapter includes daily scripture discussions from the Holy Bible (King James Version), Book of Mormon, Doctrine and Covenants, or Pearl of Great Price. And in most cases, each scripture builds on the scripture from the day before. Because of this, I highly suggest you follow the scripture discussions in order from Monday through Sunday. If you happen to miss a day, it's okay. You could double up the next day or just skip it and move on.

Following the daily scripture discussions, you'll find a quote, a few thoughtful questions you can use with your family to spark conversation, and a relevant talk from leaders of the Church. Each talk selected also has a video, and often an audio file, available on lds.org for you to watch with your family during family home evening or over the weekend.

Write in this book and love it! Use it to record the conversations you have or feelings that you experience as a family. Though for convenience you'll find entire scripture verses in this book, I encourage you to open your actual scriptures and read the daily verses from your own Bible or Book of Mormon. I promise that your family will have an increase of the Spirit if you turn to these standard works each day.

Use *52 Weeks to Fortify Your Family* around the breakfast table or in the car as you drive. Or use these lessons at night before you tuck everyone into bed. Expand on them for family home evening or spend a Sunday afternoon reviewing what you've covered. Be creative. Use this book in a way that best blesses and fortifies your family.

Value Lessons

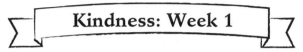

Kindness: Week 1

Daily Scripture Discussions

Monday

Our Lord has always been kind to us. He loves us and shows us mercy.

Isaiah 63:7: "I will mention the lovingkindnesses of the Lord, and the praises of the Lord, according to all that the Lord hath bestowed on us, and the great goodness toward the house of Israel, which he hath bestowed on them according to his mercies, and according to the multitude of his lovingkindnesses."

Tuesday

Treat others not as they treat you but as you would like to be treated. This is often referred to as "The Golden Rule."

3 Nephi 14:12: "Therefore, all things whatsoever ye would that men should do to you, do ye even so to them, for this is the law and the prophets."

Matthew 7:12: "Therefore all things whatsoever ye would that men should do to you, do ye even so to them: for this is the law and the prophets."

Wednesday

It's important to be kind and forgive others, as we ourselves have been forgiven.

Ephesians 4:32: "And be ye kind one to another, tenderhearted, forgiving one another, even as God for Christ's sake hath forgiven you."

Thursday

Giving to others and having a generous spirit is also a form of kindness.

Luke 6:38: "Give, and it shall be given unto you; good measure, pressed down, and shaken together, and running over, shall men give into your bosom. For with the same measure that ye mete withal it shall be measured to you again."

Friday

Jesus Christ set the example for us, showing us we even need to be kind to our enemies. *Luke 6:35:* "But love ye your enemies, and do good, and lend, hoping for nothing again; and your reward shall be great, and ye shall be the children of the Highest: for he is kind unto the unthankful and to the evil."

Saturday

We can show our neighbors—even strangers—love and kindness. We can go the extra mile to care for someone who is in need, as we learn in the story of the good Samaritan.

Luke 10:29–36: "But he, willing to justify himself, said unto Jesus, And who is my neighbour?

"And Jesus answering said, A certain man went down from Jerusalem to Jericho, and fell among thieves, which stripped him of his raiment, and wounded him, and departed, leaving him half dead.

"And by chance there came down a certain priest that way: and when he saw him, he passed by on the other side.

"And likewise a Levite, when he was at the place, came and looked on him, and passed by on the other side.

"But a certain Samaritan, as he journeyed, came where he was: and when he saw him, he had compassion on him,

"And went to him, and bound up his wounds, pouring in oil and wine, and set him on his own beast, and brought him to an inn, and took care of him.

"And on the morrow when he departed, he took out two pence, and gave them to the host, and said unto him, Take care of him; and whatsoever thou spendest more, when I come again, I will repay thee.

"Which now of these three, thinkest thou, was neighbour unto him that fell among the thieves?"

Sunday

Kindness is an important quality of charity.

Moroni 7:45: "And charity suffereth long, and is kind, and envieth not, and is not puffed up, seeketh not her own, is not easily provoked, thinketh no evil, and rejoiceth not in iniquity but rejoiceth in the truth, beareth all things, believeth all things, hopeth all things, endureth all things."

1 Corinthians 13:4: "Charity suffereth long, and is kind; charity envieth not; charity vaunteth not itself, is not puffed up."

Quote

"Kindness is the language which the deaf can hear and the blind can see."

—Mark Twain (author)

Thoughtful Questions

- Have you felt the Lord's kindness in your life?
- Do you think it is hard to be kind to your enemies?
- Do you think you should even be kind to people who bully you?
- What does the story of the good Samaritan mean to you?
- Have you ever had a chance to be like the Samaritan?

Supporting Conference Address

Joseph B. Wirthlin, "The Virtue of Kindness," *Ensign*, May 2005.

Charity: Week 2

Daily Scripture Discussions

Monday

What is charity? It is "the pure love of Christ" and the "bond of perfectness."

Moroni 7:47: "But charity is the pure love of Christ, and it endureth forever; and whoso is found possessed of it at the last day, it shall be well with him."

Colossians 3:14: "And above all these things put on charity, which is the bond of perfectness."

Tuesday

We learned in Week 1 that a trait of charity is kindness, but it has other qualities too.

Moroni 7:45: "And charity suffereth long, and is kind, and envieth not, and is not puffed up, seeketh not her own, is not easily provoked, thinketh no evil, and rejoiceth not in iniquity but rejoiceth in the truth, beareth all things, believeth all things, hopeth all things, endureth all things."

1 Corinthians 13:4–8: "Charity suffereth long, and is kind; charity envieth not; charity vaunteth not itself, is not puffed up,

"Doth not behave itself unseemly, seeketh not her own, is not easily provoked, thinketh no evil;

"Rejoiceth not in iniquity, but rejoiceth in the truth;

"Beareth all things, believeth all things, hopeth all things, endureth all things.

"Charity never faileth: but whether there be prophecies, they shall fail; whether there be tongues, they shall cease; whether there be knowledge, it shall vanish away."

Wednesday

Charity is the greatest of all and without it, "ye are nothing."

Moroni 7:46: "Wherefore, my beloved brethren, if ye have not charity, ye are nothing, for charity never faileth. Wherefore, cleave unto charity, which is the greatest of all, for all things must fail."

1 Peter 4:8: "And above all things have fervent charity among yourselves: for charity shall cover the multitude of sins."

Thursday

In addition to faith and hope, charity is necessary for us to be admitted into heaven and to have exaltation with the Lord.

Moroni 10:21: "And except ye have charity ye can in nowise be saved in the kingdom of God; neither can ye be saved in the kingdom of God if ye have not faith; neither can ye if ye have no hope."

Friday

We should strive to do all things with charity.

D&C 121:45: "Let thy bowels also be full of charity towards all men, and to the household of faith, and let virtue garnish thy thoughts unceasingly; then shall thy confidence wax strong in the presence of God; and the doctrine of the priesthood shall distil upon thy soul as the dews from heaven."

1 Corinthians 16:14: "Let all your things be done with charity."

Saturday

Jesus Christ is the perfect example of charity. He was always doing good wherever He went while on the earth. He healed the sick, blessed those in need, and preached the gospel to all who would hear.

Acts 10:38: "How God anointed Jesus of Nazareth with the Holy Ghost and with power: who went about doing good, and healing all that were oppressed of the devil; for God was with him."

Matthew 4:23: "And Jesus went about all Galilee, teaching in their synagogues, and preaching the gospel of the kingdom, and healing all manner of sickness and all manner of disease among the people."

Sunday

The Atonement of Jesus Christ is His ultimate expression of charity.

John 15:13: "Greater love hath no man than this, that a man lay down his life for his friends."

Quote

"True charity is the desire to be useful to others with no thought of recompense."

—Emanuel Swedenborg (scientist, inventor, and philosopher)

Thoughtful Questions

- What does charity mean to you?
- Can you think of a time someone has shown charity toward you?
- Do you remember a time you have had charity toward another?
- How is the Atonement of Jesus Christ an act of love?

Supporting Conference Address

Gene R. Cook, "Charity: Perfect and Everlasting Love," *Ensign*, May 2002.

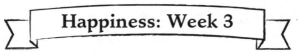

Happiness: Week 3

Daily Scripture Discussions

Monday

God created us to live and have joy. He wants us to experience happiness, no matter how hard things may be.

2 Nephi 2:25: "Adam fell that men might be; and men are, that they might have joy."

2 Nephi 2:13: "And if ye shall say there is no law, ye shall also say there is no sin. If ye shall say there is no sin, ye shall also say there is no righteousness. And if there be no righteousness there be no happiness. And if there be no righteousness nor happiness there be no punishment nor misery. And if these things are not there is no God. And if there is no God we are not, neither the earth; for there could have been no creation of things, neither to act nor to be acted upon; wherefore, all things must have vanished away."

Tuesday

Heavenly Father wants us to find true happiness. His plan for our salvation is often called "the great plan of happiness."

Alma 42:8: "Now behold, it was not expedient that man should be reclaimed from this temporal death, for that would destroy the great plan of happiness."

Wednesday

Keeping the commandments and being obedient to the Lord brings happiness into our lives.

Mosiah 2:41: "And moreover, I would desire that ye should consider on the blessed and happy state of those that keep the commandments of God. For behold, they are blessed in all things, both temporal and spiritual; and if they hold out faithful to the end they are received into heaven, that thereby they may dwell with God in a state of never-ending happiness. O remember, remember that these things are true; for the Lord God hath spoken it."

Proverbs 29:18: "Where there is no vision, the people perish: but he that keepeth the law, happy is he."

Thursday

Trusting in the Lord also brings us happiness.

Proverbs 16:20: "He that handleth a matter wisely shall find good: and whoso trusteth in the Lord, happy is he."

Friday

What if we are struggling or unhappy? We can turn to God, endure our trials, and find joy.

D&C 136:29: "If thou art sorrowful, call on the Lord thy God with supplication, that your souls may be joyful."

James 5:11: "Behold, we count them happy which endure. Ye have heard of the patience of Job, and have seen the end of the Lord; that the Lord is very pitiful, and of tender mercy."

Saturday

Many people look for happiness outside the commandments. But rejecting God's plan will not bring happiness. Satan wants you to be unhappy and miserable, as he is.

2 Nephi 2:27: "Wherefore, men are free according to the flesh; and all things are given them which are expedient unto man. And they are free to choose liberty and eternal life, through the great Mediator of all men, or to choose captivity and death, according to the captivity and power of the devil; for he seeketh that all men might be miserable like unto himself."

Alma 41:10: "Do not suppose, because it has been spoken concerning restoration, that ye shall be restored from sin to happiness. Behold, I say unto you, wickedness never was happiness."

Sunday

Your happiness can be contagious. As you choose to be happy, others may desire to know the source of your joy.

Matthew 5:16: "Let your light so shine before men, that they may see your good works, and glorify your Father which is in heaven."

Quote

"Happiness is not something ready made. It comes from your own actions."

—Dalai Lama (head monk of Tibetan Buddhism)

Thoughtful Questions

- What do trust, obedience, and endurance all have in common?
- How can following rules (being obedient) bring you happiness?
- What other things bring happiness in your life?
- How is happiness different from pleasure?

Supporting Conference Address

W. Eugene Hansen, "The Search for Happiness," *Ensign*, November 1993.

Honesty: Week 4

Daily Scripture Discussions

Monday

Honesty means being truthful and sincere at all times. The Lord delights in honesty and honest people.

D&C 97:8: "Verily I say unto you, all among them who know their hearts are honest, and are broken, and their spirits contrite, and are willing to observe their covenants by sacrifice—yea, every sacrifice which I, the Lord, shall command—they are accepted of me."

Tuesday

We should always strive to do what is honest. Dealing honestly with others is actually a commandment.

D&C 51:9: "And let every man deal honestly, and be alike among this people, and receive alike, that ye may be one, even as I have commanded you."

2 Corinthians 13:7–8: "Now I pray to God that ye do no evil; not that we should appear approved, but that ye should do that which is honest, though we be as reprobates.

"For we can do nothing against the truth, but for the truth."

Wednesday

Always speaking the truth is important, especially speaking truthfully about others.

Proverbs 24:28: "Be not a witness against thy neighbour without cause; and deceive not with thy lips."

1 Peter 3:10: "For he that will love life, and see good days, let him refrain his tongue from evil, and his lips that they speak no guile."

Thursday

We can be honest not only in our words but also in our actions.

Mosiah 4:28: "And I would that ye should remember, that whosoever among you borroweth of his neighbor should return the thing that he borroweth, according as he doth agree, or else thou shalt commit sin; and perhaps thou shalt cause thy neighbor to commit sin also."

Exodus 23:4–5: "If thou meet thine enemy's ox or his ass going astray, thou shalt surely bring it back to him again.

"If thou see the ass of him that hateth thee lying under his burden, and wouldest forbear to help him, thou shalt surely help with him."

Friday

The Lord doesn't like liars. It has been taught that there is no place for liars in heaven.

2 Nephi 9:34: "Wo unto the liar, for he shall be thrust down to hell."

Proverbs 12:22: "Lying lips are abomination to the Lord: but they that deal truly are his delight."

Saturday

Pleasing the Lord with our honest words and deeds is important. It's also important to have an honest reputation with others.

D&C 136:20: "Seek ye; and keep all your pledges one with another; and covet not that which is thy brother's."

2 Corinthians 8:21: "Providing for honest things, not only in the sight of the Lord, but also in the sight of men."

Sunday

Not sure what is honest or true? Ask to be taught through the Spirit. The Holy Ghost always speaks the truth.

Jacob 4:13: "Behold, my brethren, he that prophesieth, let him prophesy to the understanding of men; for the Spirit speaketh the truth and lieth not. Wherefore, it speaketh of things as they really are, and of things as they really will be; wherefore, these things are manifested unto us plainly, for the salvation of our souls. But behold, we are not witnesses alone in these things; for God also spake them unto prophets of old."

Quote

"Honesty is the first chapter in the book of wisdom."

—Thomas Jefferson (American Founding Father)

Thoughtful Questions

- Do you find it tough to be honest? If yes, why?
- How does gossip relate to being honest?
- When you choose to be honest (especially when it's easier to be dishonest), how do you feel?
- What do you think or feel when someone is honest with you?
- Have you ever had an experience where the Holy Ghost helped you know truth?

Supporting Conference Address

James E. Faust, "Honesty—a Moral Compass," *Ensign*, November 1996.

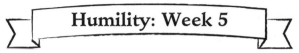

Humility: Week 5

Daily Scripture Discussions

Monday

Humility is gratefully recognizing your dependence on the Lord and desiring to do His will. A humble person acknowledges that their talents and abilities—and even weaknesses—come from God.

Ether 12:27: "And if men come unto me I will show unto them their weakness. I give unto men weakness that they may be humble; and my grace is sufficient for all men that humble themselves before me; for if they humble themselves before me, and have faith in me, then will I make weak things become strong unto them."

Tuesday

Humility is a qualification for baptism.

D&C 20:37: "And again, by way of commandment to the church concerning the manner of baptism—All those who humble themselves before God, and desire to be baptized, and come forth with broken hearts and contrite spirits, and witness before the church that they have truly repented of all their sins, and are willing to take upon them the name of Jesus Christ, having a determination to serve him to the end, and truly manifest by their works that they have received of the Spirit of Christ unto the remission of their sins, shall be received by baptism into his church."

Wednesday

We can humble ourselves through prayer and even fasting, as did David.

D&C 136:32: "Let him that is ignorant learn wisdom by humbling himself and calling upon the Lord his God, that his eyes may be opened that he may see, and his ears opened that he may hear."

Psalm 35:13: "But as for me, when they were sick, my clothing was sackcloth: I humbled my soul with fasting; and my prayer returned into mine own bosom."

Thursday

Jesus and King Benjamin taught us to be meek and to humble ourselves "as a little child."

Matthew 18:4: "Whosoever therefore shall humble himself as this little child, the same is greatest in the kingdom of heaven."

Mosiah 3:19: "For the natural man is an enemy to God, and has been from the fall of Adam, and will be, forever and ever, unless he yields to the enticings of the Holy Spirit, and putteth off the natural man and becometh a saint through the atonement of Christ the Lord, and becometh as a child, submissive, meek, humble, patient, full of love, willing to submit to all things which the Lord seeth fit to inflict upon him, even as a child doth submit to his father."

Friday

We are blessed with God's presence when we humble ourselves before Him.

D&C 112:10: "Be thou humble; and the Lord thy God shall lead thee by the hand, and give thee answer to thy prayers."

D&C 67:10: "And again, verily I say unto you that it is your privilege, and a promise I give unto you that have been ordained unto this ministry, that inasmuch as you strip yourselves from jealousies and fears, and humble yourselves before me, for ye are not sufficiently humble, the veil shall be rent and you shall see me and know that I am—not with the carnal neither natural mind, but with the spiritual."

Saturday

Humility prepares us to meet God, and through that humility we are exalted.

Alma 5:27–28: "Have ye walked, keeping yourselves blameless before God? Could ye say, if ye were called to die at this time, within yourselves, that ye have been sufficiently humble? That your garments have been cleansed and made white through the blood of Christ, who will come to redeem his people from their sins?

"Behold, are ye stripped of pride? I say unto you, if ye are not ye are not prepared to meet God. Behold ye must prepare quickly; for the kingdom of heaven is soon at hand, and such an one hath not eternal life."

Sunday

Even Jesus Christ had to humble himself before God, showing His desire to do His Father's will.

Philippians 2:8: "And being found in fashion as a man, he humbled himself, and became obedient unto death, even the death of the cross."

Luke 23:46: "And when Jesus had cried with a loud voice, he said, Father, into thy hands I commend my spirit: and having said thus, he gave up the ghost."

Quote

"Humility is not thinking less of yourself, it's thinking of yourself less."

—C. S. Lewis (novelist and theologian)

Thoughtful Questions

- What does it mean to humble yourself "as a little child"?
- How does sincere prayer humble us?
- Is it okay to "be proud" of something you did?
- Can you be humble and still be successful?
- What are the benefits of humility?

Supporting Conference Address

Marlin K. Jensen, "'To Walk Humbly with Thy God,'" *Ensign*, May 2001.

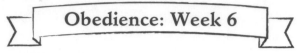

Obedience: Week 6

Daily Scripture Discussions

Monday

We learn through the plan of salvation that our existence here on earth involves a time of testing. Our goal is to show our willingness to obey Heavenly Father and keep His commandments.

Abraham 3:24–25: "And there stood one among them that was like unto God, and he said unto those who were with him: We will go down, for there is space there, and we will take of these materials, and we will make an earth whereon these may dwell;

"And we will prove them herewith, to see if they will do all things whatsoever the Lord their God shall command them."

Tuesday

Following rules and keeping commandments can often feel like a burden, even a limit to our freedom. Jesus Christ taught that true freedom comes from obedience.

John 8:31–32: "Then said Jesus to those Jews which believed on him, If ye continue in my word, then are ye my disciples indeed;

"And ye shall know the truth, and the truth shall make you free."

Wednesday

Obedience also leads to blessings from God and increased happiness.

D&C 130:20–21: "There is a law, irrevocably decreed in heaven before the foundations of this world, upon which all blessings are predicated—

"And when we obtain any blessing from God, it is by obedience to that law upon which it is predicated."

Mosiah 2:41: "And moreover, I would desire that ye should consider on the blessed and happy state of those that keep the commandments of God. For behold, they are blessed in all things, both temporal and spiritual; and if they hold out faithful to the end they are received into heaven, that thereby they may dwell with God in a state of never-ending happiness. O remember, remember that these things are true; for the Lord God hath spoken it."

Thursday

We can choose to obey the Lord's commandments and faithfully know the Lord will provide a way for us to do what He has commanded.

1 Nephi 3:7: "And it came to pass that I, Nephi, said unto my father: I will go and do the things which the Lord hath commanded, for I know that the Lord giveth no commandments unto the children of men, save he shall prepare a way for them that they may accomplish the thing which he commandeth them."

Friday

Live by the words of God.

Matthew 4:4: "But he answered and said, It is written, Man shall not live by bread alone, but by every word that proceedeth out of the mouth of God."

Saturday

Obedience to our parents is also a commandment.

Mosiah 13:20: "Honor thy father and thy mother, that thy days may be long upon the land which the Lord thy God giveth thee."

Sunday

The story of Noah is a great example from the Bible of obedience to the commandments of the Lord.

Genesis 6:22: "Thus did Noah; according to all that God commanded him, so did he."

Quote

"Obedience is the mother of success and is wedded to safety."

—Aeschylus (Greek tragedian)

Thoughtful Questions

- Do you ever feel like it's too much or too hard to be obedient?
- Can you think of a time obedience brought you happiness?
- Which is harder: obeying God or obeying your parents? Are they the same thing?
- What other scripture stories teach us about obedience?

Supporting Conference Address

Thomas S. Monson, "Obedience Brings Blessings," *Ensign*, May 2013.

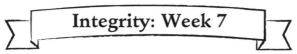

Integrity: Week 7

Daily Scripture Discussions

Monday

Do you wonder what integrity means? Helaman's stripling warriors showed us exactly the traits that integrity embodies.

Alma 53:20–21: "And they were all young men, and they were exceedingly valiant for courage, and also for strength and activity; but behold, this was not all—they were men who were true at all times in whatsoever thing they were entrusted.

"Yea, they were men of truth and soberness, for they had been taught to keep the commandments of God and to walk uprightly before him."

Tuesday

We can also learn about integrity from Job.

Job 27:5: "God forbid that I should justify you: till I die I will not remove mine integrity from me."

Wednesday

Job also showed us that we can have integrity, even in adversity.

Job 2:3–10: "And the Lord said unto Satan, Hast thou considered my servant Job, that there is none like him in the earth, a perfect and an upright man, one that feareth God, and escheweth evil? and still he holdeth fast his integrity, although thou movedst me against him, to destroy him without cause.

"And Satan answered the Lord, and said, Skin for skin, yea, all that a man hath will he give for his life.

"But put forth thine hand now, and touch his bone and his flesh, and he will curse thee to thy face.

"And the Lord said unto Satan, Behold, he is in thine hand; but save his life.

"So went Satan forth from the presence of the Lord, and smote Job with sore boils from the sole of his foot unto his crown.

"And he took him a potsherd to scrape himself withal; and he sat down among the ashes.

"Then said his wife unto him, Dost thou still retain thine integrity? curse God, and die.

"But he said unto her, Thou speakest as one of the foolish women speaketh. What? shall we receive good at the hand of God, and shall we not receive evil? In all this did not Job sin with his lips."

Thursday

Integrity is a quality God loves in His children.

D&C 124:15: "And again, verily I say unto you, blessed is my servant Hyrum Smith; for I, the Lord, love him because of the integrity of his heart, and because he loveth that which is right before me, saith the Lord."

Friday

The Lord trusts his servants whose hearts are filled with integrity.

D&C 124:20: "And again, verily I say unto you, my servant George Miller is without guile; he may be trusted because of the integrity of his heart; and for the love which he has to my testimony I, the Lord, love him."

Saturday

We can set an example of integrity for others.

Proverbs 11:3: "The integrity of the upright shall guide them: but the perverseness of transgressors shall destroy them."

Sunday

Others in our lives will be blessed when we have integrity.

Proverbs 20:7: "The just man walketh in his integrity: his children are blessed after him."

Quote

"Real integrity is doing the right thing, knowing that nobody's going to know whether you did it or not."

—Oprah Winfrey (philanthropist)

Thoughtful Questions

- Is there a difference between honesty and integrity?
- Can you remember a time when you held your integrity? Do you hold integrity in your heart always?
- Have you ever helped others keep their integrity?
- How might others in your life receive blessings from your integrity?

Supporting Conference Address

Carol B. Thomas, "Integrity," *Ensign*, May 2000.

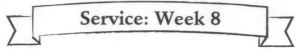

Service: Week 8

Daily Scripture Discussions

Monday

We can choose to serve the Lord.

Joshua 24:15: "And if it seem evil unto you to serve the Lord, choose you this day whom ye will serve; whether the gods which your fathers served that were on the other side of the flood, or the gods of the Amorites, in whose land ye dwell: but as for me and my house, we will serve the Lord."

Tuesday

True disciples of Jesus Christ desire to love—and likewise serve—those around them, friends and strangers alike.

John 13:35: "By this shall all men know that ye are my disciples, if ye have love one to another."

Wednesday

As we serve others, we can look to our humble Savior as our example.

Luke 22:27: "For whether is greater, he that sitteth at meat, or he that serveth? is not he that sitteth at meat? but I am among you as he that serveth."

Thursday

Just as Jesus Christ served us, we are never too good or too important to serve others.

John 13:14–16: "If I then, your Lord and Master, have washed your feet; ye also ought to wash one another's feet.

"For I have given you an example, that ye should do as I have done to you.

"Verily, verily, I say unto you, The servant is not greater than his lord; neither he that is sent greater than he that sent him."

Friday

When we serve others, we are also serving our God.

Mosiah 2:17: "And behold, I tell you these things that ye may learn wisdom; that ye may learn that when ye are in the service of your fellow beings ye are only in the service of your God."

Matthew 25:40: "And the King shall answer and say unto them, Verily I say unto you, Inasmuch as ye have done it unto one of the least of these my brethren, ye have done it unto me."

Saturday

Our extra blessings and opportunities increase our requirement to serve others.

D&C 82:3: "For of him unto whom much is given much is required; and he who sins against the greater light shall receive the greater condemnation."

Sunday

Serve with all your heart.

D&C 4:2: "Therefore, O ye that embark in the service of God, see that ye serve him with all your heart, might, mind and strength, that ye may stand blameless before God at the last day."

Quote

"The best way to find yourself is to lose yourself in the service of others."

—Mahatma Gandhi (Indian independence movement leader)

Thoughtful Questions

- What other things do people serve if they don't serve God?
- Why does the Lord need us to help others?
- How can you better serve others because of the blessings you currently have?

- Can you serve others without your whole heart?
- What did you do for someone yesterday?

Supporting Conference Address

Thomas S. Monson, "What Have I Done for Someone Today?," *Ensign*, November 2009.

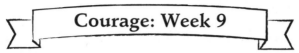

Courage: Week 9

Daily Scripture Discussions

Monday

Courage is choosing to be strong (physically, spiritually, and emotionally), true, and valiant, just as the stripling warriors were.

Alma 53:20: "And they were all young men, and they were exceedingly valiant for courage, and also for strength and activity; but behold, this was not all—they were men who were true at all times in whatsoever thing they were entrusted."

Alma 56:45: "And now I say unto you, my beloved brother Moroni, that never had I seen so great courage, nay, not amongst all the Nephites."

Tuesday

Looking at Ruth's choices and example, we can see that courage is also a "steadfastness of mind."

Ruth 1:18: "When she saw that she was steadfastly minded to go with her, then she left speaking unto her."

Wednesday

Turn to God first, thanking Him. Courage will follow.

Acts 28:15: "And from thence, when the brethren heard of us, they came to meet us as far as Appii forum, and The three taverns: whom when Paul saw, he thanked God, and took courage."

Thursday

Be patient; the Lord will strengthen your heart.

Psalm 27:14: "Wait on the Lord: be of good courage, and he shall strengthen thine heart: wait, I say, on the Lord."

Friday

You can take courage in the fact that God is with you, especially when you are in His service.

Deuteronomy 31:6: "Be strong and of a good courage, fear not, nor be afraid of them: for the Lord thy God, he it is that doth go with thee; he will not fail thee, nor forsake thee."

1 Chronicles 28:20: "And David said to Solomon his son, Be strong and of good courage, and do it: fear not, nor be dismayed: for the Lord God, even my God, will be with thee; he will not fail thee, nor forsake thee, until thou hast finished all the work for the service of the house of the Lord."

Saturday

God did not give us the spirit of fear.

2 Timothy 1:7: "For God hath not given us the spirit of fear; but of power, and of love, and of a sound mind."

Sunday

Courageously keep the commandments.

Joshua 1:7: "Only be thou strong and very courageous, that thou mayest observe to do according to all the law, which Moses my servant commanded thee: turn not from it to the right hand or to the left, that thou mayest prosper whithersoever thou goest."

Quote

"Courage is what it takes to stand up and speak; courage is also what it takes to sit down and listen."

—Winston Churchill (former prime minister of the United Kingdom)

Thoughtful Questions

- What does courage mean to you?
- Is it hard to have courage?
- In what ways can you show courage?
- How can you courageously keep the commandments at school?

Supporting Conference Address

Thomas S. Monson, "Be Strong and of a Good Courage," *Ensign*, May 2014.

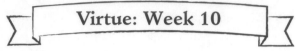

Virtue: Week 10

Daily Scripture Discussions

Monday

Virtue means having high moral standards, both in our thoughts and behaviors. Let's begin with virtuous thoughts.

D&C 121:45: "Let thy bowels also be full of charity towards all men, and to the household of faith, and let virtue garnish thy thoughts unceasingly; then shall thy confidence wax strong in the presence of God; and the doctrine of the priesthood shall distil upon thy soul as the dews from heaven."

Philippians 4:8: "Finally, brethren, whatsoever things are true, whatsoever things are honest, whatsoever things are just, whatsoever things are pure, whatsoever things are lovely, whatsoever things are of good report; if there be any virtue, and if there be any praise, think on these things."

Tuesday

In addition to virtuous thoughts, it's important to act with high moral standards. Both Emma Smith and Ruth were great examples. Through Joseph Smith, the Lord revealed the importance of virtue to Emma Smith.

D&C 25:2: "A revelation I give unto you concerning my will; and if thou art faithful and walk in the paths of virtue before me, I will preserve thy life, and thou shalt receive an inheritance in Zion."

Ruth 3:11: "And now, my daughter, fear not; I will do to thee all that thou requirest: for all the city of my people doth know that thou art a virtuous woman."

Wednesday

Virtue includes chastity and moral purity. Your body is a temple of the Holy Ghost.

1 Corinthians 6:18–20: "Flee fornication. Every sin that a man doeth is without the body; but he that committeth fornication sinneth against his own body.

"What? know ye not that your body is the temple of the Holy Ghost which is in you, which ye have of God, and ye are not your own?

"For ye are bought with a price: therefore glorify God in your body, and in your spirit, which are God's."

Thursday

We live in a wicked world, but we can remain clean and be an example to those around us.

D&C 38:42: "And go ye out from among the wicked. Save yourselves. Be ye clean that bear the vessels of the Lord. Even so. Amen."

Friday

If we have clean hands and a pure heart, we can stand with God and we will receive blessings for our virtue.

Psalm 24:3–5: "Who shall ascend into the hill of the Lord? or who shall stand in his holy place?

"He that hath clean hands, and a pure heart; who hath not lifted up his soul unto vanity, nor sworn deceitfully.

"He shall receive the blessing from the Lord, and righteousness from the God of his salvation."

Saturday

Husbands should be one with their wives. Virtue is priceless.

Genesis 2:24: "Therefore shall a man leave his father and his mother, and shall cleave unto his wife: and they shall be one flesh."

Proverbs 31:10: "Who can find a virtuous woman? for her price is far above rubies."

Sunday

Keep the Spirit with you and follow the promptings of the Holy Ghost so that you can remain clean in thought and deed.

Galatians 5:16–17: "This I say then, Walk in the Spirit, and ye shall not fulfil the lust of the flesh.

"For the flesh lusteth against the Spirit, and the Spirit against the flesh: and these are contrary the one to the other: so that ye cannot do the things that ye would."

Quote

"I hope I shall possess firmness and virtue enough to maintain what I consider the most enviable of all titles, the character of an honest man."

—George Washington (first president of the United States)

Thoughtful Questions

- Why do you think virtue begins with our thoughts?
- Is it hard to be virtuous?
- Who is an example of virtue in your life?
- What are some blessings—both temporal and eternal—you might receive from being chaste and virtuous?

Supporting Conference Address

Elaine S. Dalton, "A Return to Virtue," *Ensign*, November 2008.

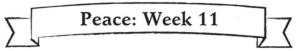

Peace: Week 11

Daily Scripture Discussions

Monday

The absence of conflict is actually not enough to bring peace. God brings peace into our lives.

1 Corinthians 14:33: "For God is not the author of confusion, but of peace, as in all churches of the saints."

Tuesday

Peace comes through the Atonement of Jesus Christ.

John 16:33: "These things I have spoken unto you, that in me ye might have peace. In the world ye shall have tribulation: but be of good cheer; I have overcome the world."

Wednesday

Even during times of trial and turmoil, we can feel peace through the ministration of the Holy Ghost.

John 14:26–27: "But the Comforter, which is the Holy Ghost, whom the Father will send in my name, he shall teach you all things, and bring all things to your remembrance, whatsoever I have said unto you.

"Peace I leave with you, my peace I give unto you: not as the world giveth, give I unto you. Let not your heart be troubled, neither let it be afraid."

Thursday

Those who love the law and are obedient have peace.

Psalm 119:165: "Great peace have they which love thy law: and nothing shall offend them."

Friday

Just as being righteous and following the Lord's commandments bring us happiness, it also brings peace. There is no peace for the wicked.

1 Nephi 20:22: "And notwithstanding he hath done all this, and greater also, there is no peace, saith the Lord, unto the wicked."

Saturday

We have a choice to be the keeper of our peace. Don't let Satan have a place in your heart to destroy your peace.

2 Nephi 4:27–28: "And why should I yield to sin, because of my flesh? Yea, why should I give way to temptations, that the evil one have place in my heart to destroy my peace and afflict my soul? Why am I angry because of mine enemy?

"Awake, my soul! No longer droop in sin. Rejoice, O my heart, and give place no more for the enemy of my soul."

Sunday

Let us seek after things that bring peace into our lives.

Romans 14:19: "Let us therefore follow after the things which make for peace, and things wherewith one may edify another."

Quote

"Peace cannot be kept by force; it can only be achieved by understanding."

—Albert Einstein (theoretical physicist)

Thoughtful Questions

- What does peace feel like for you?
- Can you think of a time when your life was crazy or upsetting and you still felt peace?

- How can we use the Atonement of Jesus Christ to find peace throughout our lives?
- What are ways we can let Satan take away our peace?

Supporting Conference Address

Paul V. Johnson, "Where Can I Turn for Peace?," *Ensign*, April 2013.

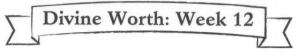

Divine Worth: Week 12

Daily Scripture Discussions

Monday

We are beloved spirit children of heavenly parents—sons and daughters of God.

Romans 8:16–17: "The Spirit itself beareth witness with our spirit, that we are the children of God:

"And if children, then heirs; heirs of God, and joint-heirs with Christ."

Tuesday

We were created in God's image and have a physical body, just like Him.

Moses 6:9: "In the image of his own body, male and female, created he them, and blessed them, and called their name Adam, in the day when they were created and became living souls in the land upon the footstool of God."

D&C 130:22: "The Father has a body of flesh and bones as tangible as man's; the Son also; but the Holy Ghost has not a body of flesh and bones, but is a personage of Spirit. Were it not so, the Holy Ghost could not dwell in us."

Wednesday

You have a divine nature and destiny. The Lord knows you personally and individually.

Jeremiah 1:5: "Before I formed thee in the belly I knew thee; and before thou camest forth out of the womb I sanctified thee, and I ordained thee a prophet unto the nations."

Thursday

You are of infinite value and worth to our Heavenly Father.

D&C 18:10: "Remember the worth of souls is great in the sight of God."

Friday

Every single soul—lost or found—is precious.

D&C 18:15: "And if it so be that you should labor all your days in crying repentance unto this people, and bring, save it be one soul unto me, how great shall be your joy with him in the kingdom of my Father!"

Saturday

Because of our divine lineage, we are entitled to promises and blessings if we remain worthy.

2 Peter 1:3–4: "According as his divine power hath given unto us all things that pertain unto life and godliness, through the knowledge of him that hath called us to glory and virtue:

"Whereby are given unto us exceeding great and precious promises: that by these ye might be partakers of the divine nature, having escaped the corruption that is in the world through lust."

1 Corinthians 2:9: "But as it is written, Eye hath not seen, nor ear heard, neither have entered into the heart of man, the things which God hath prepared for them that love him."

Sunday

What qualities would we have if we were true to our divine nature and did not fall short of our potential?

Alma 7:23–24: "And now I would that ye should be humble, and be submissive and gentle; easy to be entreated; full of patience and long-suffering; being temperate in all things; being diligent in keeping the commandments of God at all times; asking for whatsoever things ye stand in need, both spiritual and temporal; always returning thanks unto God for whatsoever things ye do receive.

"And see that ye have faith, hope, and charity, and then ye will always abound in good works."

Quote

"The Divine Light is always in man, presenting itself to the senses and to the comprehension, but man rejects it."

—Giordano Bruno (sixteenth-century philosopher)

Thoughtful Questions

- What do you think about your heavenly parents?
- In what ways do you know your Heavenly Father loves you?
- How can we see and treat others as God sees them?

Supporting Conference Address

Dieter F. Uchtdorf, "You Matter to Him," *Ensign*, November 2011.

Life Lessons

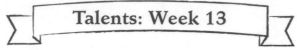

Talents: Week 13

Daily Scripture Discussions

Monday

We learn a great deal about talents from Jesus's parable of the talents. We have all been given talents, with some being given more talents than others.

Matthew 25:14–18: "For the kingdom of heaven is as a man travelling into a far country, who called his own servants, and delivered unto them his goods.

"And unto one he gave five talents, to another two, and to another one; to every man according to his several ability; and straightway took his journey.

"Then he that had received the five talents went and traded with the same, and made them other five talents.

"And likewise he that had received two, he also gained other two.

"But he that had received one went and digged in the earth, and hid his lord's money."

Tuesday

As the parable continued, Jesus taught that it matters not how many talents we have but what we do with our talents.

Matthew 25:19–25: "After a long time the lord of those servants cometh, and reckoneth with them.

"And so he that had received five talents came and brought other five talents, saying, Lord, thou deliveredst unto me five talents: behold, I have gained beside them five talents more.

"His lord said unto him, Well done, thou good and faithful servant: thou hast been faithful over a few things, I will make thee ruler over many things: enter thou into the joy of thy lord.

"He also that had received two talents came and said, Lord, thou deliveredst unto me two talents: behold, I have gained two other talents beside them.

"His lord said unto him, Well done, good and faithful servant; thou hast been faithful over a few things, I will make thee ruler over many things: enter thou into the joy of thy lord.

"Then he which had received the one talent came and said, Lord, I knew thee that thou art an hard man, reaping where thou hast not sown, and gathering where thou hast not strawed:

"And I was afraid, and went and hid thy talent in the earth: lo, there thou hast that is thine."

Wednesday

We are actually commanded to use our time wisely and not bury our talent.

D&C 60:13: "Behold, they have been sent to preach my gospel among the congregations of the wicked; wherefore, I give unto them a commandment, thus: Thou shalt not idle away thy time, neither shalt thou bury thy talent that it may not be known."

1 Timothy 4:14: "Neglect not the gift that is in thee, which was given thee by prophecy, with the laying on of the hands of the presbytery."

Thursday

Fear is often the number one thing that keeps us from using our talents.

D&C 60:2: "But with some I am not well pleased, for they will not open their mouths, but they hide the talent which I have given unto them, because of the fear of man. Wo unto such, for mine anger is kindled against them."

Friday

We can grow our talents or gain other talents and use them to benefit others, especially our Heavenly Father.

D&C 82:18–19: "And all this for the benefit of the church of the living God, that every man may improve upon his talent, that every man may gain other talents, yea, even an hundred fold, to be cast into the Lord's storehouse, to become the common property of the whole church—

"Every man seeking the interest of his neighbor, and doing all things with an eye single to the glory of God."

Saturday

It's important to keep an eye toward our Savior and avoid using our talents for evil. *Moroni 10:30:* "And again I would exhort you that ye would come unto Christ, and lay hold upon every good gift, and touch not the evil gift, nor the unclean thing."

Sunday

With talents come weaknesses. With the Lord's help, our weakness and fallen nature can be overcome.

Ether 12:27: "And if men come unto me I will show unto them their weakness. I give unto men weakness that they may be humble; and my grace is sufficient for all men that humble themselves before me; for if they humble themselves before me, and have faith in me, then will I make weak things become strong unto them."

Quote

"Use what talents you possess; the woods would be very silent if no birds sang there except those that sang best."

—Henry Van Dyke (author)

Thoughtful Questions

- What happens when we ignore our gifts or talents?
- Is there a difference between burying your talents and neglecting them?

- Has fear already stopped you from using your talents? When?
- How can we gain new talents?
- If talents are good, is it really possible to use our talents for bad things?

Supporting Conference Address

Carol B. Thomas, "Developing Our Talent for Spirituality," *Ensign*, May 2001.

Bonus Video

"The Parable of the Talents" at biblevideos.org.

Knowledge and Learning: Week 14

Daily Scripture Discussions

Monday

It's important to learn good things by studying and by having faith in what we learn. *D&C 88:118:* "And as all have not faith, seek ye diligently and teach one another words of wisdom; yea, seek ye out of the best books words of wisdom; seek learning, even by study and also by faith."

Tuesday

Learn of Jesus Christ.

D&C 19:23: "Learn of me, and listen to my words; walk in the meekness of my Spirit, and you shall have peace in me."

Matthew 11:29: "Take my yoke upon you, and learn of me; for I am meek and lowly in heart: and ye shall find rest unto your souls."

Wednesday

An understanding of and respect for the Lord is the beginning of knowledge. *Proverbs 1:7:* "The fear of the Lord is the beginning of knowledge: but fools despise wisdom and instruction."

Thursday

It is our spirit that gains knowledge and seeks learning. *Alma 18:35:* "And a portion of that Spirit dwelleth in me, which giveth me knowledge, and also power according to my faith and desires which are in God."

Friday

What we learn on earth, we keep with us in heaven. The more we learn while here on earth, the greater the advantage we will have in heaven.

D&C 130:18–19: "Whatever principle of intelligence we attain unto in this life, it will rise with us in the resurrection.

"And if a person gains more knowledge and intelligence in this life through his diligence and obedience than another, he will have so much the advantage in the world to come."

Saturday

In the Old Testament, Daniel and other young Hebrews were trained in the court of Nebuchadnezzar and were offered meat and wine. Daniel asked for a better diet for their bodies. Because of this, God blessed them with great knowledge and wisdom beyond others.

Daniel 1:8, 14–15, 17: "But Daniel purposed in his heart that he would not defile himself with the portion of the king's meat, nor with the wine which he drank: therefore he requested of the prince of the eunuchs that he might not defile himself.

"So he consented to them in this matter, and proved them ten days.

"And at the end of ten days their countenances appeared fairer and fatter in flesh than all the children which did eat the portion of the king's meat.

"As for these four children, God gave them knowledge and skill in all learning and wisdom: and Daniel had understanding in all visions and dreams."

Sunday

A wise person always seeks for more wisdom.

Proverbs 9:9: "Give instruction to a wise man, and he will be yet wiser: teach a just man, and he will increase in learning."

Quote

"Tell me and I forget. Teach me and I remember. Involve me and I learn."

—Benjamin Franklin (inventor and American Founding Father)

Thoughtful Questions

- Why do you think learning about God and Jesus Christ is "the beginning of knowledge" (Proverbs 1:7)?
- What do you think is the relationship between a healthy body and a healthy mind?
- What are three things you'd like to learn more about?

Supporting Conference Address

Mary N. Cook, "Seek Learning: You Have a Work to Do," *Ensign*, May 2012.

Trials and Adversity: Week 15

Daily Scripture Discussions

Monday

During trials or adversity it is easy for us to complain like Laman, Lemuel, and even Lehi did when they were in the wilderness without food.

1 Nephi 16:20: "And it came to pass that Laman and Lemuel and the sons of Ishmael did begin to murmur exceedingly, because of their sufferings and afflictions in the wilderness; and also my father began to murmur against the Lord his God; yea, and they were all exceedingly sorrowful, even that they did murmur against the Lord."

Tuesday

Even without food and with broken bows, Nephi stayed true to the Lord and did all that he could do to improve his situation. During our trials, it's important for us to do the same—always seeking the Lord and taking action toward a solution.

1 Nephi 16:23: "And it came to pass that I, Nephi, did make out of wood a bow, and out of a straight stick, an arrow; wherefore, I did arm myself with a bow and an arrow, with a sling and with stones. And I said unto my father: Whither shall I go to obtain food?"

Wednesday

When faced with adversity, we should trust in Heavenly Father and Jesus Christ.

Alma 36:3: "And now, O my son Helaman, behold, thou art in thy youth, and therefore, I beseech of thee that thou wilt hear my words and learn of me; for I do know that whosoever shall put their trust in God shall be supported in their trials, and their troubles, and their afflictions, and shall be lifted up at the last day."

Proverbs 3:5–6: "Trust in the Lord with all thine heart; and lean not unto thine own understanding.

"In all thy ways acknowledge him, and he shall direct thy paths."

Thursday

As we trust the Lord during trials, we can remember the blessings we are promised.

D&C 58:2–4: "For verily I say unto you, blessed is he that keepeth my commandments, whether in life or in death; and he that is faithful in tribulation, the reward of the same is greater in the kingdom of heaven.

"Ye cannot behold with your natural eyes, for the present time, the design of your God concerning those things which shall come hereafter, and the glory which shall follow after much tribulation.

"For after much tribulation come the blessings. Wherefore the day cometh that ye shall be crowned with much glory; the hour is not yet, but is nigh at hand."

Friday

It is possible to find peace even during times of trials and sadness.

John 14:27: "Peace I leave with you, my peace I give unto you: not as the world giveth, give I unto you. Let not your heart be troubled, neither let it be afraid."

Saturday

Heavenly Father and Jesus Christ will lighten our burdens and strengthen us in times of need.

Mosiah 24:15: "And now it came to pass that the burdens which were laid upon Alma and his brethren were made light; yea, the Lord did strengthen them that they could bear up their burdens with ease, and they did submit cheerfully and with patience to all the will of the Lord."

Philippians 4:13: "I can do all things through Christ which strengtheneth me."

Sunday

It's important to remember that all things work together for our good, especially our trials.

D&C 90:24: "Search diligently, pray always, and be believing, and all things shall work together for your good, if ye walk uprightly and remember the covenant wherewith ye have covenanted one with another."

Quote

"All the adversity I've had in my life, all my troubles and obstacles, have strengthened me. . . . You may not realize it when it happens, but a kick in the teeth may be the best thing in the world for you."

—Walt Disney (filmmaker)

Thoughtful Questions

- Are you currently facing a trial?
- Is it easy to trust the Lord when we are struggling?
- How can we feel peace even when our life is painful?
- Have you ever had an experience where you used the Atonement of Jesus Christ to lift your burdens?

Supporting Conference Address

Rafael E. Pino, "Faith in Adversity," *Ensign*, May 2009.

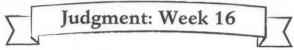

Judgment: Week 16

Daily Scripture Discussions

Monday

Some judgments are necessary. The Lord has given many commandments that we cannot keep without making righteous judgments.

D&C 38:42: "And go ye out from among the wicked. Save yourselves. Be ye clean that bear the vessels of the Lord. Even so. Amen."

Matthew 7:15–17: "Beware of false prophets, which come to you in sheep's clothing, but inwardly they are ravening wolves.

"Ye shall know them by their fruits. Do men gather grapes of thorns, or figs of thistles?

"Even so every good tree bringeth forth good fruit; but a corrupt tree bringeth forth evil fruit."

Tuesday

Judgment is an important use of your agency, and your judgments must be guided by righteous standards and used with great care, especially when you are judging other people.

Moroni 7:18–19: "And now, my brethren, seeing that ye know the light by which ye may judge, which light is the light of Christ, see that ye do not judge wrongfully; for with that same judgment which ye judge ye shall also be judged.

"Wherefore, I beseech of you, brethren, that ye should search diligently in the light of Christ that ye may know good from evil; and if ye will lay hold upon every good thing, and condemn it not, ye certainly will be a child of Christ."

1 Kings 3:9: "Give therefore thy servant an understanding heart to judge thy people, that I may discern between good and bad: for who is able to judge this thy so great a people?"

Wednesday

As Alma taught his son Corianton, it's important to be merciful, compassionate, and just as we judge others. In the Old Testament, the Lord told Zechariah the same thing.

Alma 41:14: "Therefore, my son, see that you are merciful unto your brethren; deal justly, judge righteously, and do good continually; and if ye do all these things then shall ye receive your reward; yea, ye shall have mercy restored unto you again; ye shall have justice restored unto you again; ye shall have a righteous judgment restored unto you again; and ye shall have good rewarded unto you again."

Zechariah 7:9: "Thus speaketh the Lord of hosts, saying, Execute true judgment, and shew mercy and compassions every man to his brother."

Thursday

In God's eyes, we are all equal. He does not care about our social status, origin of birth, or financial worth.

Acts 10:34–35: "Then Peter opened his mouth, and said, Of a truth I perceive that God is no respecter of persons:

"But in every nation he that feareth him, and worketh righteousness, is accepted with him."

Friday

Rather than wrongly judge someone by their appearance or life situation, we should use the Lord as an example and look at their heart.

1 Samuel 16:7: "But the Lord said unto Samuel, Look not on his countenance, or on the height of his stature; because I have refused him: for the Lord seeth not as man seeth; for man looketh on the outward appearance, but the Lord looketh on the heart."

Saturday

Let us help each other rather than judge each other.

Romans 14:12–13: "So then every one of us shall give account of himself to God.

"Let us not therefore judge one another any more: but judge this rather, that no man put a stumblingblock or an occasion to fall in his brother's way."

Sunday

After death, we are accountable and judged for our own sins.

D&C 101:78: "That every man may act in doctrine and principle pertaining to futurity, according to the moral agency which I have given unto him, that every man may be accountable for his own sins in the day of judgment."

Quote

"How easy it is to judge rightly after one sees what evil comes from judging wrongly!"

—Elizabeth Gaskell (nineteenth-century novelist)

Thoughtful Questions

- What are some important choices you will make in life that require righteous judgments such as friends, government officials, and eternal companions?
- How do you unknowingly judge people at school?
- What can you do if you have judged someone inaccurately?
- What does it mean to you to "be fair"?

Supporting Conference Address

Gregory A. Schwitzer, "Developing Good Judgment and Not Judging Others," *Ensign*, May 2010.

Wealth and Riches: Week 17

Daily Scripture Discussions

Monday

Riches and wealth are gifts from God.

Ecclesiastes 5:19: "Every man also to whom God hath given riches and wealth, and hath given him power to eat thereof, and to take his portion, and to rejoice in his labour; this is the gift of God."

Tuesday

Seek first the kingdom of God, and choose to do good things with your money.

Jacob 2:18–19: "But before ye seek for riches, seek ye for the kingdom of God.

"And after ye have obtained a hope in Christ ye shall obtain riches, if ye seek them; and ye will seek them for the intent to do good—to clothe the naked, and to feed the hungry, and to liberate the captive, and administer relief to the sick and the afflicted."

Wednesday

Money is not evil; money is necessary to help others. However, the *love* of money is evil.

1 Timothy 6:10: "For the love of money is the root of all evil: which while some coveted after, they have erred from the faith, and pierced themselves through with many sorrows."

Thursday

Jesus taught during the Sermon on the Mount that our heart can be found in the things that are important to us.

Matthew 6:19–21: "Lay not up for yourselves treasures upon earth, where moth and rust doth corrupt, and where thieves break through and steal:

"But lay up for yourselves treasures in heaven, where neither moth nor rust doth corrupt, and where thieves do not break through nor steal:

"For where your treasure is, there will your heart be also."

Friday

In the book of Genesis, Jacob covenanted to pay tithes. Because all we have comes from God, we too can give back a tenth to the Lord.

Genesis 28:22: "And this stone, which I have set for a pillar, shall be God's house: and of all that thou shalt give me I will surely give the tenth unto thee."

Saturday

Because the Nephites were faithful to the Lord and His commandments, they prospered, just as they'd been promised. During their prosperous times and circumstances, they chose to help, serve, and bless everyone in need.

Alma 1:29–31: "And now, because of the steadiness of the church they began to be exceedingly rich, having abundance of all things whatsoever they stood in need—an abundance of flocks and herds, and fatlings of every kind, and also abundance of grain, and of gold, and of silver, and of precious things, and abundance of silk and fine-twined linen, and all manner of good homely cloth.

"And thus, in their prosperous circumstances, they did not send away any who were naked, or that were hungry, or that were athirst, or that were sick, or that had not been nourished; and they did not set their hearts upon riches; therefore they were liberal to all, both old and young, both bond and free, both male and female, whether out of the church or in the church, having no respect to persons as to those who stood in need.

"And thus they did prosper and become far more wealthy than those who did not belong to their church."

Sunday

But we must be careful of the "pride cycle." Within just a few years these Nephites we just learned about were already caught up in pride. (Well over ten times in the Book of Mormon do prophets warn about problems of pride relating to the nature of clothing.)

Alma 4:6: "And it came to pass in the eighth year of the reign of the judges, that the people of the church began to wax proud, because of their exceeding riches, and their fine silks, and their fine-twined linen, and because of their many flocks and herds, and their gold and their silver, and all manner of precious things, which they had obtained by their industry; and in all these things were they lifted up in the pride of their eyes, for they began to wear very costly apparel."

Quote

"The test of our progress is not whether we add more to the abundance of those who have much; it is whether we provide enough for those who have too little."

Franklin D. Roosevelt (former president of the United States)

Thoughtful Questions

- Have you seen financial blessings from the Lord?
- If you had more money, what ways would you help others?
- What is the difference between wants and needs?
- How can we avoid the "pride cycle"?

Supporting Conference Address

Joe J. Christensen, "Greed, Selfishness, and Overindulgence," *Ensign*, May 1999.

Gospel Lessons

Godhead: Week 18

Daily Scripture Discussions

Monday

We believe God, Jesus Christ, and the Holy Ghost make up the Godhead and are three separate beings.

Articles of Faith 1:1: "We believe in God, the Eternal Father, and in His Son, Jesus Christ, and in the Holy Ghost."

Tuesday

"The true doctrine of the Godhead was lost in the Apostasy that followed the Savior's mortal ministry and the deaths of His Apostles. This doctrine began to be restored when 14-year-old Joseph Smith received his First Vision" (*True to the Faith: A Gospel Reference* [2004], 73).

Joseph Smith—History 1:17: "It no sooner appeared than I found myself delivered from the enemy which held me bound. When the light rested upon me I saw two Personages, whose brightness and glory defy all description, standing above me in the air. One of them spake unto me, calling me by name and said, pointing to the other—This is My Beloved Son. Hear Him!"

Wednesday

Heavenly Father and Jesus Christ have bodies like ours.

D&C 130:22: "The Father has a body of flesh and bones as tangible as man's; the Son also; but the Holy Ghost has not a body of flesh and bones, but is a personage of Spirit. Were it not so, the Holy Ghost could not dwell in us."

Thursday

We receive the gift of the Holy Ghost when we are baptized.

Moses 6:52: "And he also said unto him: If thou wilt turn unto me, and hearken unto my voice, and believe, and repent of all thy transgressions, and be baptized, even in water, in the name of mine Only Begotten Son, who is full of grace and truth, which is Jesus Christ, the only name which shall be given under heaven, whereby salvation shall come unto the children of men, ye shall receive the gift of the Holy Ghost, asking all things in his name, and whatsoever ye shall ask, it shall be given you."

Friday

Even though the Godhead is made up of distinct individuals with distinct roles, They are of one purpose.

D&C 35:2: "I am Jesus Christ, the Son of God, who was crucified for the sins of the world, even as many as will believe on my name, that they may become the sons of God, even one in me as I am one in the Father, as the Father is one in me, that we may be one."

John 17:21: "That they all may be one; as thou, Father, art in me, and I in thee, that they also may be one in us: that the world may believe that thou hast sent me."

Saturday

The Godhead's singular purpose is bringing to pass Heavenly Father's plan of salvation, which is the eternal exaltation and joy of all who accept Them.

Mormon 7:5–7: "Know ye that ye must come to the knowledge of your fathers, and repent of all your sins and iniquities, and believe in Jesus Christ, that he is the Son of God, and that he was slain by the Jews, and by the power of the Father he hath risen again, whereby he hath gained the victory over the grave; and also in him is the sting of death swallowed up.

"And he bringeth to pass the resurrection of the dead, whereby man must be raised to stand before his judgment-seat.

"And he hath brought to pass the redemption of the world, whereby he that is found guiltless before him at the judgment day hath it given unto him to dwell in the presence of God in his kingdom, to sing ceaseless praises with the choirs above, unto the Father, and unto the Son, and unto the Holy Ghost, which are one God, in a state of happiness which hath no end."

Sunday

We can seek eternal life and personally come to know each member of the Godhead. *2 Nephi 31:18:* "And then are ye in this strait and narrow path which leads to eternal life; yea, ye have entered in by the gate; ye have done according to the commandments of the Father and the Son; and ye have received the Holy Ghost, which witnesses of the Father and the Son, unto the fulfilling of the promise which he hath made, that if ye entered in by the way ye should receive."

Quote

"The revelations of the Father and the Son are conveyed through the third member of the Godhead, even the Holy Ghost. The Holy Ghost is the witness of and messenger for the Father and the Son."

—David A. Bednar (member of the Quorum of the Twelve Apostles)

Thoughtful Questions

- Should you respect your body more, knowing you are created in God's image?
- What do promptings from the Holy Ghost feel like for you?
- How can you draw closer to Jesus Christ?

Supporting Conference Address

Gordon B. Hinckley, "The Father, Son, and Holy Ghost," *Ensign*, November 1986.

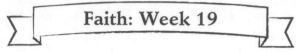

Faith: Week 19

Daily Scripture Discussions

Monday

The Apostle Paul taught us what faith is, as did Alma in the Book of Mormon.

Hebrews 11:1: "Now faith is the substance of things hoped for, the evidence of things not seen."

Alma 32:21: "And now as I said concerning faith—faith is not to have a perfect knowledge of things; therefore if ye have faith ye hope for things which are not seen, which are true."

Tuesday

Faith is a principle of action and power.

Moroni 7:33: "And Christ hath said: If ye will have faith in me ye shall have power to do whatsoever thing is expedient in me."

Wednesday

Our Savior, Jesus Christ, is the cornerstone of faith, leading to our salvation.

Enos 1:8: "And he said unto me: Because of thy faith in Christ, whom thou hast never before heard nor seen. And many years pass away before he shall manifest himself in the flesh; wherefore, go to, thy faith hath made thee whole."

Thursday

Often our faith is challenged. Those trials of our faith make us strong and are precious.

Ether 12:6: "And now, I, Moroni, would speak somewhat concerning these things; I would show unto the world that faith is things which are hoped for and not seen; wherefore, dispute not because ye see not, for ye receive no witness until after the trial of your faith."

1 Peter 1:7: "That the trial of your faith, being much more precious than of gold that perisheth, though it be tried with fire, might be found unto praise and honour and glory at the appearing of Jesus Christ."

Friday

Miracles are possible according to our faith.

2 Nephi 26:13: "And that he manifesteth himself unto all those who believe in him, by the power of the Holy Ghost; yea, unto every nation, kindred, tongue, and people, working mighty miracles, signs, and wonders, among the children of men according to their faith."

Matthew 9:28–29: "And when he was come into the house, the blind men came to him: and Jesus saith unto them, Believe ye that I am able to do this? They said unto him, Yea, Lord.

"Then touched he their eyes, saying, According to your faith be it unto you."

Saturday

Even a small amount of faith can move mountains.

Matthew 17:20: "And Jesus said unto them, Because of your unbelief: for verily I say unto you, If ye have faith as a grain of mustard seed, ye shall say unto this mountain, Remove hence to yonder place; and it shall remove; and nothing shall be impossible unto you."

Sunday

We can increase our faith by studying the scriptures and keeping the commandants.

Alma 32:27: "But behold, if ye will awake and arouse your faculties, even to an experiment upon my words, and exercise a particle of faith, yea, even if ye can no more than desire to believe, let this desire work in you, even until ye believe in a manner that ye can give place for a portion of my words."

Quote

"Faith is about doing. You are how you act, not just how you believe."
—Mitch Albom (author of *Have a Little Faith: A True Story*)

Thoughtful Questions

- How is faith an "action" word?
- Is it hard to believe in something you have not seen?
- What miracles have you seen because of your faith?
- How can faith grow like a seed?

Supporting Conference Address

Richard C. Edgley, "Faith—the Choice Is Yours," *Ensign*, November 2010.

Repentance: Week 20

Daily Scripture Discussions

Monday

Our sins make us unworthy to return and live with our Heavenly Father.

Alma 11:37: "And I say unto you again that he cannot save them in their sins; for I cannot deny his word, and he hath said that no unclean thing can inherit the kingdom of heaven; therefore, how can ye be saved, except ye inherit the kingdom of heaven? Therefore, ye cannot be saved in your sins."

Tuesday

Thankfully we can repent of our sins and try again.

Ezra 10:11: "Now therefore make confession unto the Lord God of your fathers, and do his pleasure: and separate yourselves from the people of the land, and from the strange wives."

Wednesday

We should not procrastinate our repentance.

Alma 34:32–33: "For behold, this life is the time for men to prepare to meet God; yea, behold the day of this life is the day for men to perform their labors.

"And now, as I said unto you before, as ye have had so many witnesses, therefore, I beseech of you that ye do not procrastinate the day of your repentance until the end; for after this day of life, which is given us to prepare for eternity, behold, if we do not improve our time while in this life, then cometh the night of darkness wherein there can be no labor performed."

Thursday

If we don't repent, we will perish and not receive eternal life.

1 Nephi 14:5: "And it came to pass that the angel spake unto me, Nephi, saying: Thou hast beheld that if the Gentiles repent it shall be well with them; and thou also knowest concerning the covenants of the Lord unto the house of Israel; and thou also hast heard that whoso repenteth not must perish."

Friday

Godly sorrow is necessary for repentance.

2 Corinthians 7:10: "For godly sorrow worketh repentance to salvation not to be repented of: but the sorrow of the world worketh death."

Saturday

Repentance leads to forgiveness, and the Lord forgets our sins (unless we repeat them).

Jeremiah 31:34: "And they shall teach no more every man his neighbour, and every man his brother, saying, Know the Lord: for they shall all know me, from the least of them unto the greatest of them, saith the Lord: for I will forgive their iniquity, and I will remember their sin no more."

D&C 58:42: "Behold, he who has repented of his sins, the same is forgiven, and I, the Lord, remember them no more."

D&C 82:7: "And now, verily I say unto you, I, the Lord, will not lay any sin to your charge; go your ways and sin no more; but unto that soul who sinneth shall the former sins return, saith the Lord your God."

Sunday

Repent of your sins and sin no more!

D&C 58:43: "By this ye may know if a man repenteth of his sins—behold, he will confess them and forsake them."

John 5:14: "Afterward Jesus findeth him in the temple, and said unto him, Behold, thou art made whole: sin no more, lest a worse thing come unto thee."

Quote

"The heavens will not be filled with those who never made mistakes but with those who recognized that they were off course and who corrected their ways to get back in the light of gospel truth."

—Dieter F. Uchtdorf (member of the First Presidency)

Thoughtful Questions

- Why do you think we make mistakes?
- Why can't we return to Heavenly Father if we don't repent?
- How do we say we are sorry? How do we repent of sins?
- How often do we need to repent?

Supporting Conference Address

Neil L. Andersen, "Repent . . . That I May Heal You," *Ensign*, November 2009.

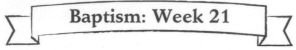

Baptism: Week 21

Daily Scripture Discussions

Monday

Baptism is the first saving ordinance of the gospel.

Articles of Faith 1:4: "We believe that the first principles and ordinances of the Gospel are: first, Faith in the Lord Jesus Christ; second, Repentance; third, Baptism by immersion for the remission of sins; fourth, Laying on of hands for the gift of the Holy Ghost."

Tuesday

As an example, Jesus Christ was baptized even though He was without sin.

Matthew 3:13–17: "Then cometh Jesus from Galilee to Jordan unto John, to be baptized of him.

"But John forbad him, saying, I have need to be baptized of thee, and comest thou to me?

"And Jesus answering said unto him, Suffer it to be so now: for thus it becometh us to fulfil all righteousness. Then he suffered him.

"And Jesus, when he was baptized, went up straightway out of the water: and, lo, the heavens were opened unto him, and he saw the Spirit of God descending like a dove, and lighting upon him:

"And lo a voice from heaven, saying, This is my beloved Son, in whom I am well pleased."

Wednesday

We covenant with God when we are baptized. We promise to serve Him, keep His commandments, and take upon ourselves the name of Jesus Christ.

Mosiah 18:8–9: "And it came to pass that he said unto them: Behold, here are the waters of Mormon (for thus were they called) and now, as ye are desirous to come into the fold of God, and to be called his people, and are willing to bear one another's burdens, that they may be light;

"Yea, and are willing to mourn with those that mourn; yea, and comfort those that stand in need of comfort, and to stand as witnesses of God at all times and in all things, and in all places that ye may be in, even until death, that ye may be redeemed of God, and be numbered with those of the first resurrection, that ye may have eternal life."

Thursday

The Savior revealed to the Prophet Joseph Smith the true order of baptism. Baptism must be by immersion, performed by someone with priesthood authority.

D&C 20:73–74: "The person who is called of God and has authority from Jesus Christ to baptize, shall go down into the water with the person who has presented himself or herself for baptism, and shall say, calling him or her by name: Having been commissioned of Jesus Christ, I baptize you in the name of the Father, and of the Son, and of the Holy Ghost. Amen.

"Then shall he immerse him or her in the water, and come forth again out of the water."

Friday

Little children have no need for baptism until they reach the age of accountability.

D&C 29: 46–47: "But behold, I say unto you, that little children are redeemed from the foundation of the world through mine Only Begotten;

"Wherefore, they cannot sin, for power is not given unto Satan to tempt little children, until they begin to become accountable before me."

D&C 68:27: "And their children shall be baptized for the remission of their sins when eight years old, and receive the laying on of the hands."

Saturday

After baptism, you are confirmed a member and given the gift of the Holy Ghost.

D&C 49:13–14: "Repent and be baptized in the name of Jesus Christ, according to the holy commandment, for the remission of sins;

"And whoso doeth this shall receive the gift of the Holy Ghost, by the laying on of the hands of the elders of the church."

Sunday

We will receive eternal life if we endure to the end and keep our covenants, including those we make at baptism.

2 Nephi 31:17–18: "Wherefore, do the things which I have told you I have seen that your Lord and your Redeemer should do; for, for this cause have they been shown unto me, that ye might know the gate by which ye should enter. For the gate by which ye should enter is repentance and baptism by water; and then cometh a remission of your sins by fire and by the Holy Ghost.

"And then are ye in this strait and narrow path which leads to eternal life; yea, ye have entered in by the gate; ye have done according to the commandments of the Father and the Son; and ye have received the Holy Ghost, which witnesses of the Father and the Son, unto the fulfilling of the promise which he hath made, that if ye entered in by the way ye should receive."

Quote

"[Baptism] is a sign and a commandment which God has set for man to enter into His kingdom. Those who seek to enter in any other way will seek in vain; for God will not receive them, neither will the angels acknowledge their works as accepted, for they have not obeyed the ordinances, nor attended to the signs which God ordained for the salvation of man, to prepare him for, and give him a title to, a celestial glory."

—Joseph Smith (first President of the Church)

Thoughtful Questions

- Why do you think it was important for Jesus to set an example for us?
- What do you remember about your baptism?
- How can you keep the covenants you made at baptism?

Supporting Conference Address

Robert D. Hales, "The Covenant of Baptism: To Be in the Kingdom and of the Kingdom," *Ensign*, November 2000.

Holy Ghost: Week 22

Daily Scripture Discussions

Monday

The Holy Ghost is the third member of the Godhead and does not have a body like ours. *D&C 130:22:* "The Father has a body of flesh and bones as tangible as man's; the Son also; but the Holy Ghost has not a body of flesh and bones, but is a personage of Spirit. Were it not so, the Holy Ghost could not dwell in us."

Tuesday

The Holy Ghost has many different roles within the unity of the Godhead. The Holy Ghost is a witness of God and Jesus Christ. He also helps us know all truth.

2 Nephi 31:18: "And then are ye in this strait and narrow path which leads to eternal life; yea, ye have entered in by the gate; ye have done according to the commandments of the Father and the Son; and ye have received the Holy Ghost, which witnesses of the Father and the Son, unto the fulfilling of the promise which he hath made, that if ye entered in by the way ye should receive."

Moroni 10:5: "And by the power of the Holy Ghost ye may know the truth of all things."

Wednesday

The Holy Ghost can teach, guide, protect, and comfort us.

2 Nephi 32: 2–5: "Do ye not remember that I said unto you that after ye had received the Holy Ghost ye could speak with the tongue of angels? And now, how could ye speak with the tongue of angels save it were by the Holy Ghost?

"Angels speak by the power of the Holy Ghost; wherefore, they speak the words of Christ. Wherefore, I said unto you, feast upon the words of Christ; for behold, the words of Christ will tell you all things what ye should do.

"Wherefore, now after I have spoken these words, if ye cannot understand them it will be because ye ask not, neither do ye knock; wherefore, ye are not brought into the light, but must perish in the dark.

"For behold, again I say unto you that if ye will enter in by the way, and receive the Holy Ghost, it will show unto you all things what ye should do."

John 14:26: "But the Comforter, which is the Holy Ghost, whom the Father will send in my name, he shall teach you all things, and bring all things to your remembrance, whatsoever I have said unto you."

Thursday

The Holy Ghost is also the Holy Spirit of Promise. And as so, He confirms that the priesthood ordinances and covenants you've made are acceptable to God.

D&C 132:7: "And verily I say unto you, that the conditions of this law are these: All covenants, contracts, bonds, obligations, oaths, vows, performances, connections, associations, or expectations, that are not made and entered into and sealed by the Holy Spirit of promise, of him who is anointed, both as well for time and for all eternity, and that too most holy, by revelation and commandment through the medium of mine anointed, whom I have appointed on the earth to hold this power (and I have appointed unto my servant Joseph to hold this power in the last days, and there is never but one on the earth at a time on whom this power and the keys of this priesthood are conferred), are of no efficacy, virtue, or force in and after the resurrection from the dead; for all contracts that are not made unto this end have an end when men are dead."

Ephesians 1:13: "In whom ye also trusted, after that ye heard the word of truth, the gospel of your salvation: in whom also after that ye believed, ye were sealed with that holy Spirit of promise."

Friday

After baptism, we are confirmed a member of the Church and receive the gift of the Holy Ghost.

Moses 6:52: "And he also said unto him: If thou wilt turn unto me, and hearken unto my voice, and believe, and repent of all thy transgressions, and be baptized, even in water, in the name of mine Only Begotten Son, who is full of grace and truth, which is Jesus Christ, the only name which shall be given under heaven, whereby salvation shall come unto the children of men, ye shall receive the gift of the Holy Ghost, asking all things in his name, and whatsoever ye shall ask, it shall be given you."

Acts 2:38: "Then Peter said unto them, Repent, and be baptized every one of you in the name of Jesus Christ for the remission of sins, and ye shall receive the gift of the Holy Ghost."

Saturday

We all feel the Holy Ghost differently.

D&C 84:88: "And whoso receiveth you, there I will be also, for I will go before your face. I will be on your right hand and on your left, and my Spirit shall be in your hearts, and mine angels round about you, to bear you up."

D&C 9:8: "But, behold, I say unto you, that you must study it out in your mind; then you must ask me if it be right, and if it is right I will cause that your bosom shall burn within you; therefore, you shall feel that it is right."

Acts 13:52: "And the disciples were filled with joy, and with the Holy Ghost."

Sunday

You body is a temple. To keep the Holy Ghost with you, you need to take good care of your body and make good choices.

Helaman 4:24: "And they saw that they had become weak, like unto their brethren, the Lamanites, and that the Spirit of the Lord did no more preserve them; yea, it had withdrawn from them because the Spirit of the Lord doth not dwell in unholy temples."

1 Corinthians 6:19: "What? know ye not that your body is the temple of the Holy Ghost which is in you, which ye have of God, and ye are not your own?"

Quote

"We need to know that the Lord rarely speaks loudly. His messages almost always come in a whisper."

—Dallin H. Oaks (member of the Quorum of the Twelve Apostles)

Thoughtful Questions

- Have you ever felt comfort from the Holy Ghost?
- What way(s) do you feel the Spirit?
- How could you help someone else feel the Spirit?
- When does the Holy Ghost leave us?

Supporting Conference Address

Craig C. Christensen, "An Unspeakable Gift From God," *Ensign*, November 2012.

Bonus Video

"Feeling the Holy Ghost" at lds.org in media library.

Light of Christ: Week 23

Daily Scripture Discussions

Monday

Things that are good are light, and things that are evil are darkness.

D&C 50:23–25: "And that which doth not edify is not of God, and is darkness.

"That which is of God is light; and he that receiveth light, and continueth in God, receiveth more light; and that light groweth brighter and brighter until the perfect day.

"And again, verily I say unto you, and I say it that you may know the truth, that you may chase darkness from among you."

Tuesday

Jesus Christ is the Light of the World.

D&C 11:28: "Behold, I am Jesus Christ, the Son of God. I am the life and the light of the world."

John 8:12: "Then spake Jesus again unto them, saying, I am the light of the world: he that followeth me shall not walk in darkness, but shall have the light of life."

Wednesday

Everyone is born with the Light of Christ.

John 1:9: "That was the true Light, which lighteth every man that cometh into the world."

Thursday

Conscience is a manifestation of the Light of Christ, helping us to know good from evil.

Moroni 7:16: "For behold, the Spirit of Christ is given to every man, that he may know good from evil; wherefore, I show unto you the way to judge; for every thing which inviteth to do good, and to persuade to believe in Christ, is sent forth by the power and gift of Christ; wherefore ye may know with a perfect knowledge it is of God."

Friday

The Light of Christ governs all things

D&C 88:12–13: "Which light proceedeth forth from the presence of God to fill the immensity of space—

"The light which is in all things, which giveth life to all things, which is the law by which all things are governed, even the power of God who sitteth upon his throne, who is in the bosom of eternity, who is in the midst of all things."

Saturday

We can choose to walk in the light of the Lord when we follow His words and heed His commandments.

2 Nephi 12:5: "O house of Jacob, come ye and let us walk in the light of the Lord; yea, come, for ye have all gone astray, every one to his wicked ways."

Isaiah 2:5: "O house of Jacob, come ye, and let us walk in the light of the Lord."

Sunday

Let your light shine and show the world your good works. The example you show to others has a greater impact than you know.

3 Nephi 12:16: "Therefore let your light so shine before this people, that they may see your good works and glorify your Father who is in heaven."

Quote

"Darkness cannot drive out darkness; only light can do that. Hate cannot drive out hate; only love can do that."

—Martin Luther King Jr. (civil rights activist)

Thoughtful Questions

- Do you prefer light or darkness? Why?
- Why is it important everyone gets the Light of Christ?
- How can you "let your light shine"?

Supporting Conference Address

Quentin L. Cook, "Let There Be Light!" *Ensign*, November 2010.

Plan of Salvation: Week 24

Daily Scripture Discussions

Monday

Heavenly Father prepared a plan for us to become like Him, experience great joy, and return to live with Him again. This is God's plan and is also referred to as "the plan of happiness" or "the plan of redemption."

2 Nephi 9:13: "O how great the plan of our God! For on the other hand, the paradise of God must deliver up the spirits of the righteous, and the grave deliver up the body of the righteous; and the spirit and the body is restored to itself again, and all men become incorruptible, and immortal, and they are living souls, having a perfect knowledge like unto us in the flesh, save it be that our knowledge shall be perfect."

Alma 22:13: "And Aaron did expound unto him the scriptures from the creation of Adam, laying the fall of man before him, and their carnal state and also the plan of redemption, which was prepared from the foundation of the world, through Christ, for all whosoever would believe on his name."

Tuesday

Before you were born, you lived in heaven with your Heavenly Father. You are one of His "noble and great" spirit children.

Abraham 3:22: "Now the Lord had shown unto me, Abraham, the intelligences that were organized before the world was; and among all these there were many of the noble and great ones."

D&C 93:23: "Ye were also in the beginning with the Father; that which is Spirit, even the Spirit of truth."

Wednesday

You attended a council in heaven where Heavenly Father presented his great plan of salvation. During this council, Jesus Christ (who was the Firstborn Son of the Father in the spirit) agreed to be the Savior.

Abraham 3:23–28: "And God saw these souls that they were good, and he stood in the midst of them, and he said: These I will make my rulers; for he stood among those that were spirits, and he saw that they were good; and he said unto me: Abraham, thou art one of them; thou wast chosen before thou wast born.

"And there stood one among them that was like unto God, and he said unto those who were with him: We will go down, for there is space there, and we will take of these materials, and we will make an earth whereon these may dwell;

"And we will prove them herewith, to see if they will do all things whatsoever the Lord their God shall command them;

"And they who keep their first estate shall be added upon; and they who keep not their first estate shall not have glory in the same kingdom with those who keep their first estate; and they who keep their second estate shall have glory added upon their heads for ever and ever.

"And the Lord said: Whom shall I send? And one answered like unto the Son of Man: Here am I, send me. And another answered and said: Here am I, send me. And the Lord said: I will send the first.

"And the second was angry, and kept not his first estate; and, at that day, many followed after him."

Moses 4:2: "But, behold, my Beloved Son, which was my Beloved and Chosen from the beginning, said unto me—Father, thy will be done, and the glory be thine forever."

Thursday

Right now, you are alive on earth with a physical body—the mortal experience of God's plan of salvation.

Alma 34:32: "For behold, this life is the time for men to prepare to meet God; yea, behold the day of this life is the day for men to perform their labors."

Friday

When our physical body dies, our spirit continues to live in the spirit world.

Alma 40:12: "And then shall it come to pass, that the spirits of those who are righteous are received into a state of happiness, which is called paradise, a state of rest, a state of peace, where they shall rest from all their troubles and from all care, and sorrow."

Saturday

At the time of resurrection, everyone will be resurrected. Our bodies and spirit will be reunited.

D&C 29:26: "But, behold, verily I say unto you, before the earth shall pass away, Michael, mine archangel, shall sound his trump, and then shall all the dead awake, for their graves shall be opened, and they shall come forth—yea, even all."

Alma 40:23: "The soul shall be restored to the body, and the body to the soul; yea, and every limb and joint shall be restored to its body; yea, even a hair of the head shall not be lost; but all things shall be restored to their proper and perfect frame."

Sunday

In heaven, there are three kingdoms of glory: celestial, terrestrial, and telestial.

John 14:2: "In my Father's house are many mansions: if it were not so, I would have told you. I go to prepare a place for you."

D&C 137:1: "The heavens were opened upon us, and I beheld the celestial kingdom of God, and the glory thereof, whether in the body or out I cannot tell."

D&C 76:77–78: "These are they who receive of the presence of the Son, but not of the fulness of the Father.

"Wherefore, they are bodies terrestrial, and not bodies celestial, and differ in glory as the moon differs from the sun."

Additional Reading

For the details on the kingdoms of glory, see D&C 76:50–119.

Quote

"If you understand the great plan of happiness and follow it, what goes on in the world will not determine your happiness."

—Boyd K. Packer (member of the Quorum of the Twelve Apostles)

Thoughtful Questions

- What choice did we make in the premortal existence?
- How can we implement the plan of salvation in our lives?
- How do you think this knowledge we have sets us apart from others?
- What blessings do we have from the plan of salvation?
- What choices can you make to return to live with Heavenly Father?

Supporting Conference Address

L. Tom Perry, "The Plan of Salvation," *Ensign*, November 2006.

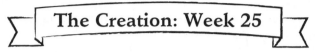

The Creation: Week 25

Daily Scripture Discussions

Monday

Under Heavenly Father's direction, Jesus Christ created the heavens and the earth.

Moses 2:1: "And it came to pass that the Lord spake unto Moses, saying: Behold, I reveal unto you concerning this heaven, and this earth. . . . I am the Beginning and the End, the Almighty God; by mine Only Begotten I created these things; yea, in the beginning I created the heaven, and the earth upon which thou standest."

Tuesday

Scripture revealed through Joseph Smith tells us that in the Creation, Jesus organized the earth from elements that already existed. He did not create it from nothing.

Abraham 3:24–25: "And there stood one among them that was like unto God, and he said unto those who were with him; We will go down, for there is space there, and we will take of these materials, and we will make an earth whereon these may dwell.

"And we will prove them herewith, to see if they will do all things whatsoever the Lord their God shall command them."

Wednesday

Each phase of the Creation was well planned before it was ever accomplished here.

Moses 3:4–5: "And now, behold, I say unto you, that these are the generations of the heaven and of the earth, when they were created, in the day that I, the Lord God, made the heaven and the earth,

"And every plant of the field before it was in the earth, and every herb of the field before it grew. For I, the Lord God, created all things, of which I have spoken, spiritually, before they were naturally upon the face of the earth. For I, the Lord God, had not caused it to rain upon the face of the earth. And I, the Lord God, had created all the children of men; and not yet a man to till the ground; for in heaven created I them; and there was not yet flesh upon the earth, neither in the water, neither in the air."

Thursday

The physical Creation was done in ordered periods of time. In Genesis and Moses, the periods are called *days*. In the book of Abraham, each period is referred to as a *time*.

Genesis 1:5: "And God called the light Day, and the darkness he called Night. And the evening and the morning were the first day."

Moses 2:5: "And I, God, called the light Day; and the darkness, I called Night; and this I did by the word of my power, and it was done as I spake; and the evening and the morning were the first day."

Abraham 4:8: "And the Gods called the expanse, Heaven. And it came to pass that it was from evening until morning that they called night; and it came to pass that it was from morning until evening that they called day; and this was the second time that they called night and day."

Friday

The earth is only one of many just like it, all of which are God's creations.

Moses 1:33: "And worlds without number have I created; and I also created them for mine own purpose; and by the Son I created them, which is mine Only Begotten."

D&C 76:23–24: "For we saw him, even on the right hand of God; and we heard the voice bearing record that he is the Only Begotten of the Father—

"That by him, and through him, and of him, the worlds are and were created, and the inhabitants thereof are begotten sons and daughters unto God."

Saturday

On the sixth day (or time), God created Adam and Eve. The earth was created for us.

Abraham 4:26–27: "And the Gods took counsel among themselves and said: Let us go down and form man in our image, after our likeness; and we will give them dominion over the fish of the sea, and over the fowl of the air, and over the cattle, and over all the earth, and over every creeping thing that creepeth upon the earth. "So the Gods went down to organize man in their own image, in the image of the Gods to form they him, male and female to form they them."

D&C 59:18: "Yea, all things which come of the earth, in the season thereof, are made for the benefit and the use of man, both to please the eye and to gladden the heart."

Sunday

This all did not happen by accident! The Creation itself testifies of a divine Creator. *Psalm 104:24:* "O Lord, how manifold are thy works! in wisdom hast thou made them all: the earth is full of thy riches."

Additional Reading

For the whole Creation story, see Genesis 1–2:3, Moses 2:3–3:3, or Abraham 4–5:3.

Quote

"While I know myself as a creation of God, I am also obligated to realize and remember that everyone else and everything else are also God's creation."—Maya Angelou (author)

Thoughtful Questions

- What things did God create?
- When you realize all of God's creations, do you treat them differently?
- Do you think it was hard for God to send us to earth?

Supporting Conference Address

Russell M. Nelson, "The Creation," *Ensign*, May 2000.

Atonement of Jesus Christ: Week 26

Daily Scripture Discussions

Monday

"The word *atone* means to reconcile, or to restore to harmony. Through the Atonement of Jesus Christ, we can be reconciled to our Heavenly Father" (*True to the Faith*, 14).

Jacob 4:11: "Wherefore, beloved brethren, be reconciled unto him through the atonement of Christ, his Only Begotten Son, and ye may obtain a resurrection, according to the power of the resurrection which is in Christ, and be presented as the first-fruits of Christ unto God, having faith, and obtained a good hope of glory in him before he manifested himself in the flesh."

Romans 5:10–11: "For if, when we were enemies, we were reconciled to God by the death of his Son, much more, being reconciled, we shall be saved by his life.

"And not only so, but we also joy in God through our Lord Jesus Christ, by whom we have now received the atonement."

Tuesday

Before the coming of Jesus, animal sacrifices were symbolic of the Atonement. In His life, he made that sacrifice in the Garden of Gethsemane and on the cross.

Moses 5:5–8: "And he gave unto them commandments, that they should worship the Lord their God, and should offer the firstlings of their flocks, for an offering unto the Lord. And Adam was obedient unto the commandments of the Lord.

"And after many days an angel of the Lord appeared unto Adam, saying : Why dost thou offer sacrifices unto the Lord? And Adam said unto him: I know not, save the Lord commanded me.

"And then the angel spake, saying: This thing is a similitude of the sacrifice of the Only Begotten of the Father, which is full of grace and truth.

"Wherefore, thou shalt do all that thou doest in the name of the Son, and thou shalt repent and call upon God in the name of the Son forevermore."

Luke 22:41–45: "And he was withdrawn from them about a stone's cast, and kneeled down, and prayed,

"Saying, Father, if thou be willing, remove this cup from me: nevertheless not my will, but thine, be done.

"And there appeared an angel unto him from heaven, strengthening him.

"And being in an agony he prayed more earnestly: and his sweat was as it were great drops of blood falling down to the ground.

"And when he rose up from prayer, and was come to his disciples, he found them sleeping for sorrow."

Wednesday

The Atonement redeems us from the Fall of Adam.

1 Corinthians 15:22: "For as in Adam all die, even so in Christ shall all be made alive."

John 3:16–17: "For God so loved the world, that he gave his only begotten Son, that whosoever believeth in him should not perish, but have everlasting life.

"For God sent not his Son into the world to condemn the world; but that the world through him might be saved."

Thursday

Jesus Christ was foreordained to come to earth, suffer for our sins, die on the cross and be resurrected. It was His will to fulfill the Father's plan.

Moses 4:2: "But, behold, my Beloved Son, which was my Beloved and Chosen from the beginning, said unto me—Father, thy will be done, and the glory be thine forever."

Ether 3:14: "Behold, I am he who was prepared from the foundation of the world to redeem my people. Behold, I am Jesus Christ. I am the Father and the Son. In me shall

all mankind have life, and that eternally, even they who shall believe on my name; and they shall become my sons and my daughters."

Friday

"Having lived a perfect, sinless life, He was free from the demands of justice" (*True to the Faith*, 16).

D&C 20:22: "He suffered temptations but gave no heed unto them."

D&C 45:4–5: "Saying: Father, behold the sufferings and death of him who did no sin, in whom thou wast well pleased; behold the blood of thy Son which was shed, the blood of him whom thou gavest that thyself might be glorified;

"Wherefore, Father, spare these my brethren that believe on my name, that they may come unto me and have everlasting life."

Saturday

Through the use of the Atonement, our sins are forgiven.

2 Nephi 2:7: "Behold, he offereth himself a sacrifice for sin, to answer the ends of the law, unto all those who have a broken heart and a contrite spirit; and unto none else can the ends of the law be answered."

Sunday

The Atonement is also available to heal us of our pain, sorrow, and any affliction.

Alma 7:11: "And he shall go forth, suffering pains and afflictions and temptations of every kind; and this that the word might be fulfilled which saith he will take upon him the pains and the sicknesses of his people."

Quote

"It wasn't a potential atonement actuated by the sinner, it was an actual atonement initiated by the Savior."

—John MacArthur (author)

Thoughtful Questions

- How can you use the Savior's Atonement in your life?
- Can you still be forgiven if you have a lot of sins?
- Can the Atonement really help with pain and sadness?

Supporting Conference Address

Richard G. Scott, "Personal Strength through the Atonement of Jesus Christ," *Ensign*, November 2013.

Bonus Video

"The Savior Suffers in Gethsemane," available at biblevideos.org.

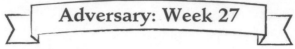

Adversary: Week 27

Daily Scripture Discussions

Monday

Satan (the devil) was also known as Lucifer and is a spirit son of God.

D&C 76:25–26, 28: "And this we saw also, and bear record, that an angel of God who was in authority in the presence of God, who rebelled against the Only Begotten Son whom the Father loved and who was in the bosom of the Father, was thrust down from the presence of God and the Son,

"And was called Perdition, for the heavens wept over him—he was Lucifer, a son of the morning.

"And while we were yet in the Spirit, the Lord commanded us that we should write the vision; for we beheld Satan, that old serpent, even the devil, who rebelled against God, and sought to take the kingdom of our God and his Christ."

Tuesday

Satan persuaded a third of the angels of heaven to turn away from the Father. They all were cast out of heaven.

D&C 29:36–37: "And it came to pass that Adam, being tempted of the devil—for, behold, the devil was before Adam, for he rebelled against me, saying, Give me thine honor, which is my power; and also a third part of the hosts of heaven turned he away from me because of their agency;

"And they were thrust down, and thus came the devil and his angels."

Revelation 12:9: "And the great dragon was cast out, that old serpent, called the Devil, and Satan, which deceiveth the whole world; he was cast out into the earth, and his angels were cast out with him."

Wednesday

As part of your mortal experience, God allows Satan and his followers to tempt you, allowing you your agency.

D&C 29:39: "And it must needs be that the devil should tempt the children of men, or they could not be agents unto themselves; for if they never should have bitter they could not know the sweet."

Thursday

Satan will try to destroy you with his temptations. He wants you to fail and be unhappy like he is.

3 Nephi 18:18: "Behold, verily, verily, I say unto you, ye must watch and pray always lest ye enter into temptation; for Satan desireth to have you, that he may sift you as wheat."

2 Nephi 2:27: "Wherefore, men are free according to the flesh; and all things are given them which are expedient unto man. And they are free to choose liberty and eternal life, through the great Mediator of all men, or to choose captivity and death, according to the captivity and power of the devil; for he seeketh that all men might be miserable like unto himself."

Friday

The devil is very subtle and cunning.

Genesis 3:1: "Now the serpent was more subtil than any beast of the field which the Lord God had made. And he said unto the woman, Yea, hath God said, Ye shall not eat of every tree of the garden?"

Alma 12:4–6: "And thou seest that we know that thy plan was a very subtle plan, as to the subtlety of the devil, for to lie and to deceive this people that thou mightest set them against us, to revile us and to cast us out—

"Now this was a plan of thine adversary, and he hath exercised his power in thee. Now I would that ye should remember that what I say unto thee I say unto all.

"And behold I say unto you all that this was a snare of the adversary, which he has laid to catch this people, that he might bring you into subjection unto him, that he might encircle you about with his chains, that he might chain you down to everlasting destruction, according to the power of his captivity."

Saturday

You always have the power in you to choose good over evil! You don't have to give into Satan's temptations. Seek the Lord's help through prayer.

Alma 34:39: "Yea, and I also exhort you, my brethren, that ye be watchful unto prayer continually, that ye may not be led away by the temptations of the devil, that he may not overpower you, that ye may not become his subjects at the last day; for behold, he rewardeth you no good thing."

Alma 13:28: "But that ye would humble yourselves before the Lord, and call on his holy name, and watch and pray continually, that ye may not be tempted above that which ye can bear, and thus be led by the Holy Spirit, becoming humble, meek, submissive, patient, full of love and all long-suffering."

Sunday

Satan will be bound during the Millennium.

D&C 88:110: "Satan shall be bound, that old serpent, who is called the devil, and shall not be loosed for the space of a thousand years."

Revelations 20:2: "And he laid hold on the dragon, that old serpent, which is the Devil, and Satan, and bound him a thousand years."

Quote

"If you don't set the tone for the day, the devil will set it for you."

—Joel Osteen (preacher)

Thoughtful Questions

- Can the devil "make" you do something? Or do you have free choice?
- Can you think of subtle ways you've been tempted?
- How can you find strength to resist Satan?
- How would Satan want you to start your day? How would God want you to start your day?

Supporting Conference Address

Richard C. Edgley, "Satan's Bag of Snipes," *Ensign*, November 2000.

Principles of Prayer: Week 28

Daily Scripture Discussions

Monday

It's important to pray regularly, both individually and as a family.

3 Nephi 18:19, 21: "Therefore ye must always pray unto the Father in my name.

"Pray in your families unto the Father, always in my name, that your wives and your children may be blessed."

Tuesday

We pray to our Heavenly Father in Jesus Christ's name.

John 14: 13–14: "And whatsoever ye shall ask in my name, that will I do, that the Father may be glorified in the Son.

"If ye shall ask any thing in my name, I will do it."

John 15:7: "If ye abide in me, and my words abide in you, ye shall ask what ye will, and it shall be done unto you."

Wednesday

Our prayers should be meaningful and felt from the heart.

Moroni 7:9: "And likewise also is it counted evil unto a man, if he shall pray and not with real intent of heart; yea, and it profiteth him nothing, for God receiveth none such."

Moroni 7:48: "Wherefore, my beloved brethren, pray unto the Father with all the energy of heart, that ye may be filled with this love, which he hath bestowed upon all who are true followers of his Son, Jesus Christ; that ye may become the sons of God; that when he shall appear we shall be like him, for we shall see him as he is; that we may have this hope; that we may be purified even as he is pure. Amen."

Matthew 6:7–8: "But when ye pray, use not vain repetitions, as the heathen do: for they think that they shall be heard for their much speaking.

"Be not ye therefore like unto them: for your Father knoweth what things ye have need of, before ye ask him."

Thursday

We should always remember to give thanks for our blessings during our prayers.

1 Thessalonians 5:18: "In every thing give thanks: for this is the will of God in Christ Jesus concerning you."

Alma 34:38: "And that ye live in thanksgiving daily, for the many mercies and blessings which he doth bestow upon you."

Friday

Then we can ask for Heavenly Father's help and guidance.

Alma 37:36–37: "Yea, and cry unto God for all thy support; yea, let all thy doings be unto the Lord, and whithersoever thou goest let it be in the Lord; yea, let all thy thoughts be directed unto the Lord; yea, let the affections of thy heart be placed upon the Lord forever.

"Counsel with the Lord in all thy doings, and he will direct thee for good; yea, when thou liest down at night lie down unto the Lord, that he may watch over you in your sleep; and when thou risest in the morning let thy heart be full of thanks unto God; and if ye do these things, ye shall be lifted up at the last day."

Saturday

When we pray, we should remember the needs of others as well.

Alma 34:27: "Yea, and when you do not cry unto the Lord, let your hearts be full, drawn out in prayer unto him continually for your welfare, and also for the welfare of those who are around you."

Sunday

It's important that we do all we can do to assist in receiving an answer to our prayers. *D&C 9:7–8:* "Behold, you have not understood; you have supposed that I would give it unto you, when you took no thought save it was to ask me.

"But, behold, I say unto you, that you must study it out in your mind; then you must ask me if it be right, and if it is right I will cause that your bosom shall burn within you; therefore, you shall feel that it is right."

Quote

"In prayer it is better to have a heart without words than words without a heart."

—Mahatma Gandhi (Indian independence movement leader)

Thoughtful Questions

- Why is it important for our prayers to start and end the same?
- What does it feel like when you sincerely pray?
- Do you think it's okay to pray silently in your head?
- How can we show respect or reverence when we pray?

Supporting Conference Address

J. Devn Cornish, "The Privilege of Prayer," *Ensign*, November 2011.

Power of Prayer: Week 29

Daily Scripture Discussions

Monday

The power of your prayers depends on you. Personal, private prayer is important to your spiritual growth.

Matthew 6:6: "But thou, when thou prayest, enter into thy closet, and when thou hast shut thy door, pray to thy Father which is in secret; and thy Father which seeth in secret shall reward thee openly."

D&C 19:28: "And again, I command thee that thou shalt pray vocally as well as in thy heart; yea, before the world as well as in secret, in public as well as in private."

Tuesday

You are always worthy to pray! Satan wants to keep you from praying and would have you believe you are unworthy to pray.

2 Nephi 32:8: "And now, my beloved brethren, I perceive that ye ponder still in your hearts; and it grieveth me that I must speak concerning this thing. For if ye would hearken unto the Spirit which teacheth a man to pray, ye would know that ye must pray; for the evil spirit teacheth not a man to pray, but teacheth him that he must not pray."

Wednesday

Prayer can protect us—and those we love—from temptation and even physical danger.

D&C 10:5: "Pray always, that you may come off conqueror; yea, that you may conquer Satan, and that you may escape the hands of the servants of Satan that do uphold his work."

Thursday

Family prayer will strengthen our family and bring us blessings. The Savior taught this principle to the Nephites.

3 Nephi 18:21: "Pray in your families unto the Father, always in my name, that your wives and your children may be blessed."

Friday

Our Heavenly Father hears our prayers and answers them in His own time.

D&C 88:64: "Whatsoever ye ask the Father in my name it shall be given unto you, that is expedient for you."

Matthew 7:7–8: "Ask, and it shall be given you; seek, and ye shall find; knock, and it shall be opened unto you:

"For every one that asketh receiveth; and he that seeketh findeth; and to him that knocketh it shall be opened."

Saturday

We receive answers to our prayers in different ways. Sometimes the Lord's answer is actually no.

D&C 112:10: "Be thou humble; and the Lord thy God shall lead thee by the hand, and give thee answer to thy prayers."

D&C 8:2: "Yea, behold, I will tell you in your mind and in your heart, by the Holy Ghost, which shall come upon you and which shall dwell in your heart."

D&C 9:9: "But if it be not right you shall have no such feelings, but you shall have a stupor of thought that shall cause you to forget the thing which is wrong; therefore, you cannot write that which is sacred save it be given you from me."

Sunday

Faith and prayer can have the power to heal.

James 5:15–16: "And the prayer of faith shall save the sick, and the Lord shall raise him up; and if he have committed sins, they shall be forgiven him.

"Confess your faults one to another, and pray one for another, that ye may be healed. The effectual fervent prayer of a righteous man availeth much."

Quote

"Prayer is not asking. Prayer is putting oneself in the hands of God, at His disposition, and listening to His voice in the depth of our hearts."

—Mother Teresa (founder of Missionaries of Charity)

Thoughtful Questions

- Has a prayer that you've said ever made you feel safe?
- When was a time the Lord answered your prayer?
- What do you think would happen if multiple people prayed for the same thing at the same time?

Supporting Conference Address

Richard G. Scott, "Using the Supernal Gift of Prayer," *Ensign*, May 2007.

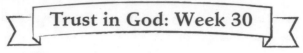

Trust in God: Week 30

Daily Scripture Discussions

Monday

Those who put their trust in God are blessed.

Helaman 12:1: "And thus we can behold how false, and also the unsteadiness of the hearts of the children of men; yea, we can see that the Lord in his great infinite goodness doth bless and prosper those who put their trust in him."

Jeremiah 17:7: "Blessed is the man that trusteth in the Lord, and whose hope the Lord is."

Tuesday

It's important to trust God with all our heart.

Proverbs 3:5–6: "Trust in the Lord with all thine heart; and lean not unto thine own understanding.

"In all thy ways acknowledge him, and he shall direct thy paths."

Wednesday

When we trust in God, He will protect us and keep us safe.

Alma 61:13: "But behold he doth not command us that we shall subject ourselves to our enemies, but that we should put our trust in him, and he will deliver us."

Proverbs 29:25: "The fear of man bringeth a snare: but whoso putteth his trust in the Lord shall be safe."

Thursday

In the Old Testament, Shadrach, Meshach, and Abed-nego were three Israelite youths who, along with Daniel, were brought into the palace of King Nebuchadnezzar. They refused to worship a golden image and were cast into a fiery furnace, and because of their trust in God, they survived! (Read Daniel 3 for the entire story.)

Daniel 3:28: "Then Nebuchadnezzar spake, and said, Blessed be the God of Shadrach, Meshach, and Abed-nego, who hath sent his angel, and delivered his servants that trusted in him, and have changed the king's word, and yielded their bodies, that they might not serve nor worship any god, except their own God."

Friday

In addition to blessings and safety, trusting in God also brings us happiness.

Proverbs 16:20: "He that handleth a matter wisely shall find good: and whoso trusteth in the Lord, happy is he."

Saturday

Don't trust in man, only God.

2 Nephi 4:34: "O Lord, I have trusted in thee, and I will trust in thee forever. I will not put my trust in the arm of flesh; for I know that cursed is he that putteth his trust in the arm of flesh. Yea, cursed is he that putteth his trust in man or maketh flesh his arm."

Psalm 20:7: "Some trust in chariots, and some in horses: but we will remember the name of the Lord our God."

Sunday

Also, don't trust in riches.

Proverbs 11:28: "He that trusteth in his riches shall fall: but the righteous shall flourish as a branch."

Quote

"It isn't as bad as you sometimes think it is.
It all works out. Don't worry.
I say that to myself every morning.
It will all work out.

Put your trust in God,
and move forward with faith
and confidence in the future."

—Gordon B. Hinckley (from the funeral program for
Marjorie Pay Hinckley, April 10, 2004)

Thoughtful Questions

- Do you think it is hard to trust in the Lord?
- How can you trust with *all* your heart?
- Can we trust in man and God at the same time?
- How do we *show* our trust?

Supporting Conference Address

Henry B. Eyring, "Trust in God, Then Go and Do," *Ensign*, November 2010.

Worship and the Sabbath: Week 31

Daily Scripture Discussions

Monday

The first commandment is to worship only God, our Heavenly Father.

Exodus 20:3: "Thou shalt have no other gods before me."

1 Nephi 17:55: "And now, they said: We know of a surety that the Lord is with thee, for we know that it is the power of the Lord that has shaken us. And they fell down before me, and were about to worship me, but I would not suffer them, saying: I am thy brother, yea, even thy younger brother; wherefore, worship the Lord thy God, and honor thy father and thy mother, that thy days may be long in the land which the Lord thy God shall give thee."

Tuesday

Satan tempts us to worship him and other things of the world.

Moses 6:49: "Behold Satan hath come among the children of men, and tempteth them to worship him; and men have become carnal, sensual, and devilish, and are shut out from the presence of God."

Wednesday

It's important to worship in holy places.

Psalm 5:7: "But as for me, I will come into thy house in the multitude of thy mercy: and in thy fear will I worship toward thy holy temple."

Alma 15:17: "Therefore, after Alma having established the church at Sidom, seeing a great check, yea, seeing that the people were checked as to the pride of their hearts, and began to humble themselves before God, and began to assemble themselves together at their sanctuaries to worship God before the altar, watching and praying continually, that they might be delivered from Satan, and from death, and from destruction."

Thursday

The Sabbath day is the Lord's day. The fourth commandment is to keep it holy.

Exodus 20:8–11: "Remember the sabbath day, to keep it holy.

"Six days shalt thou labour, and do all thy work:

"But the seventh day is the sabbath of the Lord thy God: in it thou shalt not do any work, thou, nor thy son, nor thy daughter, thy manservant, nor thy maidservant, nor thy cattle, nor thy stranger that is within thy gates:

"For in six days the Lord made heaven and earth, the sea, and all that in them is, and rested the seventh day: wherefore the Lord blessed the sabbath day, and hallowed it."

Friday

In Old Testament times, God's people observed the Sabbath on the seventh day of the week. The Resurrection of Jesus Christ occurred on the first day of the week. Because of this, the Lord's disciples began to observe the Sabbath on the first day of the week.

Acts 20:7: "And upon the first day of the week, when the disciples came together to break bread, Paul preached unto them, ready to depart on the morrow; and continued his speech until midnight."

Saturday

The Sabbath is provided to help us focus on God, not on the world. It's a day meant for prayer, worship, and rest.

D&C 59:9–10: "And that thou mayest more fully keep thyself unspotted from the world, thou shalt go to the house of prayer and offer up thy sacraments upon my holy day.

"For verily this is a day appointed unto you to rest from your labors, and to pay thy devotions unto the Most High."

Mark 2:27: "And he said unto them, The sabbath was made for man, and not man for the sabbath."

Sunday

The Lord has promised us great blessings when we observe the Sabbath day.

D&C 59:12–13, 16: "But remember that on this, the Lord's day, thou shalt offer thine oblations and thy sacraments unto the Most High, confessing thy sins unto thy brethren, and before the Lord.

"And on this day thou shalt do none other thing, only let thy food be prepared with singleness of heart that thy fasting may be perfect, or, in other words, that thy joy may be full.

"Verily I say, that inasmuch as ye do this, the fulness of the earth is yours, the beasts of the field and the fowls of the air, and that which climbeth upon the trees and walketh upon the earth."

Quote

"I never knew how to worship until I knew how to love."

—Henry Ward Beecher (nineteenth-century minister)

Thoughtful Questions

- What things might we worship more than God?
- Where is an appropriate place to worship God?
- What activities do we feel are appropriate for our family on the Sabbath?
- Can you think of a blessing you or someone you know has received from keeping the Sabbath day holy?

Supporting Conference Address

H. Aldridge Gillespie, "The Blessing of Keeping the Sabbath Day Holy," *Ensign*, November 2000.

The Sacrament: Week 32

Daily Scripture Discussions

Monday

Partaking of the sacrament is the center of our Sabbath day observance. The night before the Crucifixion, Jesus Christ met with his disciples and instituted the sacrament. *Luke 22:19–20:* "And he took bread, and gave thanks, and brake it, and gave unto them, saying, This is my body which is given for you: this do in remembrance of me. "Likewise also the cup after supper, saying, This cup is the new testament in my blood, which is shed for you."

Tuesday

When Christ was resurrected, he visited the Nephites and instituted the sacrament with them.

3 Nephi 18: 1–5: "And it came to pass that Jesus commanded his disciples that they should bring forth some bread and wine unto him.

"And while they were gone for bread and wine, he commanded the multitude that they should sit themselves down upon the earth.

"And when the disciples had come with bread and wine, he took of the bread and brake and blessed it; and he gave unto the disciples and commanded that they should eat.

"And when they had eaten and were filled, he commanded that they should give unto the multitude.

"And when the multitude had eaten and were filled, he said unto the disciples: Behold there shall one be ordained among you, and to him will I give power that he shall break bread and bless it and give it unto the people of my church, unto all those who shall believe and be baptized in my name."

Wednesday

The sacrament is an opportunity for us to remember Jesus Christ and His Atonement for us. The bread symbolizes His body and His physical suffering.

3 Nephi 18:7: "And this shall ye do in remembrance of my body, which I have shown unto you. And it shall be a testimony unto the Father that ye do always remember me. And if ye do always remember me ye shall have my Spirit to be with you."

Thursday

The small cup of water symbolizes the event in the Garden of Gethsemane where the Savior shed His blood during intense spiritual suffering.

Mosiah 3:7: "And lo, he shall suffer temptations, and pain of body, hunger, thirst, and fatigue, even more than man can suffer, except it be unto death; for behold, blood cometh from every pore, so great shall be his anguish for the wickedness and the abominations of his people."

3 Nephi 18:11: "And this shall ye always do to those who repent and are baptized in my name; and ye shall do it in remembrance of my blood, which I have shed for you, that ye may witness unto the Father that ye do always remember me. And if ye do always remember me ye shall have my Spirit to be with you."

Friday

When we partake of the sacrament, we witness to God that we remember His Son and renew our baptismal covenants.

Mosiah 18:9: "Yea, and are willing to mourn with those that mourn; yea, and comfort those that stand in need of comfort, and to stand as witnesses of God at all times and in all things, and in all places that ye may be in, even until death, that ye may be redeemed of God, and be numbered with those of the first resurrection, that ye may have eternal life."

Saturday

When we worthily partake of the sacrament, the Lord renews the promised remission of our sins.

D&C 20:77: "O God, the Eternal Father, we ask thee in the name of thy Son, Jesus Christ, to bless and sanctify this bread to the souls of all those who partake of it, that they may eat in remembrance of the body of thy Son, and witness unto thee, O God, the Eternal Father, that they are willing to take upon them the name of thy Son, and always remember him and keep his commandments which he has given them; that they may always have his Spirit to be with them. Amen."

Sunday

Each week we should humbly prepare for the sacred ordinance of the sacrament.

3 Nephi 9:20: "And ye shall offer for a sacrifice unto me a broken heart and a contrite spirit. And whoso cometh unto me with a broken heart and a contrite spirit, him will I baptize with fire and with the Holy Ghost, even as the Lamanites, because of their faith in me at the time of their conversion, were baptized with fire and with the Holy Ghost, and they knew it not."

Quote

"Windows must be washed regularly to clean away the dust and dirt. . . . Just as earthly windows need consistent, thorough cleaning, so do the windows of our spirituality. . . . By partaking of the sacrament worthily to renew our basptismal covenants, we clarify our view of life's eternal purpose and divine priorities. The sacrament prayers invite personal introspection, repentance, and rededication as we pledge our willingness to remember our Savior, Jesus the Christ."

—Joseph B. Wirthlin (member of the Quorum of the Twelve Apostles)

Thoughtful Questions

- What do you think about during the sacrament?
- What *should* we think about during the sacrament?
- What is something you can do to make the sacrament more meaningful?

Supporting Conference Address

Don R. Clarke, "Blessings of the Sacrament," *Ensign*, November 2012.

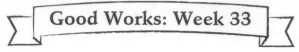

Good Works: Week 33

Daily Scripture Discussions

Monday

Show your love for others through service and good works. It is the Lord's second commandment that we love one another.

1 John 3:18: "My little children, let us not love in word, neither in tongue; but in deed and in truth."

Tuesday

Our good works are a reflection of our love for our Heavenly Father.

Matthew 5:16: "Let your light so shine before men, that they may see your good works, and glorify your Father which is in heaven."

Wednesday

We can serve and bless others on behalf of our Heavenly Father.

D&C 81:4: "And in doing these things thou wilt do the greatest good unto thy fellow beings, and wilt promote the glory of him who is your Lord."

Thursday

Don't be afraid to do good things for other people.

D&C 6:33: "Fear not to do good, my sons, for whatsoever ye sow, that shall ye also reap; therefore, if ye sow good ye shall also reap good for your reward."

Friday

We will be judged according to our good works.

Mosiah 3:24: "And thus saith the Lord: They shall stand as a bright testimony against this people, at the judgment day; whereof they shall be judged, every man according to his works, whether they be good, or whether they be evil."

Saturday

We will also be rewarded eternal blessings for our good works.

Alma 9:28: "Therefore, prepare ye the way of the Lord, for the time is at hand that all men shall reap a reward of their works, according to that which they have been—if they have been righteous they shall reap the salvation of their souls, according to the power and deliverance of Jesus Christ; and if they have been evil they shall reap the damnation of their souls, according to the power and captivation of the devil."

Mosiah 5:15: "Therefore, I would that ye should be steadfast and immovable, always abounding in good works, that Christ, the Lord God Omnipotent, may seal you his, that you may be brought to heaven, that ye may have everlasting salvation and eternal life, through the wisdom, and power, and justice, and mercy of him who created all things, in heaven and in earth, who is God above all. Amen."

Matthew 16:27: "For the Son of man shall come in the glory of his Father with his angels; and then he shall reward every man according to his works."

Sunday

You can recognize other disciples of Jesus Christ by their actions and good works.

D&C 18:38: "And by their desires and their works you shall know them."

Quote

"To be doing good deeds is man's most glorious task."

—Sophocles (Greek tragedian)

Thoughtful Questions

- How does your heart feel when you do good things for other people?
- Do you think doing a good deed for someone else makes a difference?

- Can you remember something someone did for you that made a difference, big or small?
- How are our good works really a reflection of our Savior or Heavenly Father?

Supporting Conference Address

Henry B. Eyring, "Opportunities to Do Good," *Ensign*, May 2011.

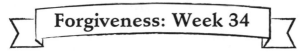

Forgiveness: Week 34

Daily Scripture Discussions

Monday

In the Lord's Prayer, Jesus counseled us to ask Heavenly Father to forgive us, as we forgive others.

Matthew 6:12: "And forgive us our debts, as we forgive our debtors."

Tuesday

We all have made mistakes and likewise have sinned.

1 John 1:8–9: "If we say that we have no sin, we deceive ourselves, and the truth is not in us.

"If we confess our sins, he is faithful and just to forgive us our sins, and to cleanse us from all unrighteousness."

Wednesday

It's important to regularly seek forgiveness from the Lord through personal prayer.

1 Nephi 7:21: "And it came to pass that I did frankly forgive them all that they had done, and I did exhort them that they would pray unto the Lord their God for forgiveness. And it came to pass that they did so. And after they had done praying unto the Lord we did again travel on our journey towards the tent of our father."

D&C 58:42: "Behold, he who has repented of his sins, the same is forgiven, and I, the Lord, remember them no more."

Thursday

The Lord is ready and waiting to forgive us. We just need to ask.

Psalm 86:5: "For thou, Lord, art good, and ready to forgive; and plenteous in mercy unto all them that call upon thee."

Friday

Part of forgiveness is also a willingness to forgive others.

D&C 64:9–10: "Wherefore, I say unto you, that ye ought to forgive one another; for he that forgiveth not his brother his trespasses standeth condemned before the Lord; for there remaineth in him the greater sin.

"I, the Lord, will forgive whom I will forgive, but of you it is required to forgive all men."

Saturday

This is perhaps the ultimate example of forgiveness: the Savior forgave the Roman soldiers who crucified Him.

Luke 23:34: "Then said Jesus, Father, forgive them; for they know not what they do. And they parted his raiment, and cast lots."

Sunday

How often must we forgive others?

D&C 98:39–40: "And again, verily I say unto you, if after thine enemy has come upon thee the first time, he repent and come unto thee praying thy forgiveness, thou shalt forgive him, and shalt hold it no more as a testimony against thine enemy—

"And so on unto the second and third time; and as oft as thine enemy repenteth of the trespass wherewith he has trespassed against thee, thou shalt forgive him, until seventy times seven."

Matthew 18:21–22: "Then came Peter to him, and said, Lord, how oft shall my brother sin against me, and I forgive him? till seven times?

"Jesus saith unto him, I say not unto thee, Until seven times: but, Until seventy times seven."

Quote

"When you forgive, you in no way change the past—but you sure do change the future."

—Bernard Meltzer (advice radio show host)

Thoughtful Questions

- What does it mean to forgive someone?
- What might happen if you don't forgive?
- What would it be like if you and I were never forgiven by family? By the Lord?

Supporting Conference Address

James E. Faust, "The Healing Power of Forgiveness," *Ensign*, May 2007.

Commandments: Week 35

Daily Scripture Discussions

Monday

God gives us commandments for our benefit and even our joy.

Deuteronomy 6:24: "And the Lord commanded us to do all these statutes, to fear the Lord our God, for our good always, that he might preserve us alive, as it is at this day."

John 15:11: "These things have I spoken unto you, that my joy might remain in you, and that your joy might be full."

Tuesday

Obedience to commandments leads to blessings from God.

D&C 130: 20–21: "There is a law, irrevocably decreed in heaven before the foundations of this world, upon which all blessings are predicated—

"And when we obtain any blessing from God, it is by obedience to that law upon which it is predicated."

Wednesday

King Benjamin taught that those who keep the commandments are happy and blessed, both temporally and spiritually.

Mosiah 2:41: "And moreover, I would desire that ye should consider on the blessed and happy state of those that keep the commandments of God. For behold, they are blessed in all things, both temporal and spiritual; and if they hold out faithful to the end they are received into heaven, that thereby they may dwell with God in a state of never-ending happiness. O remember, remember that these things are true; for the Lord God hath spoken it."

Thursday

Our obedience to the commandments is an expression of our love for Heavenly Father and Jesus Christ.

John 15:10: "If ye keep my commandments, ye shall abide in my love; even as I have kept my Father's commandments, and abide in his love."

Friday

The Lord will always prepare a way for us to keep His commandments.

1 Nephi 3:7: "And it came to pass that I, Nephi, said unto my father: I will go and do the things which the Lord hath commanded, for I know that the Lord giveth no commandments unto the children of men, save he shall prepare a way for them that they may accomplish the thing which he commandeth them."

Saturday

The Ten Commandments are eternal gospel principles that are necessary for our exaltation. The Lord revealed them to Moses in ancient times.

Exodus 20:1–17: "And God spake all these words, saying,

"I am the Lord thy God, which have brought thee out of the land of Egypt, out of the house of bondage.

"Thou shalt have no other gods before me.

"Thou shalt not make unto thee any graven image, or any likeness of any thing that is in heaven above, or that is in the earth beneath, or that is in the water under the earth:

"Thou shalt not bow down thyself to them, nor serve them: for I the Lord thy God am a jealous God, visiting the iniquity of the fathers upon the children unto the third and fourth generation of them that hate me;

"And shewing mercy unto thousands of them that love me, and keep my commandments.

"Thou shalt not take the name of the Lord thy God in vain; for the Lord will not hold him guiltless that taketh his name in vain.

"Remember the sabbath day, to keep it holy.

"Six days shalt thou labour, and do all thy work:

"But the seventh day is the sabbath of the Lord thy God: in it thou shalt not do any work, thou, nor thy son, nor thy daughter, thy manservant, nor thy maidservant, nor thy cattle, nor thy stranger that is within thy gates:

"For in six days the Lord made heaven and earth, the sea, and all that in them is, and rested the seventh day: wherefore the Lord blessed the sabbath day, and hallowed it.

"Honour thy father and thy mother: that thy days may be long upon the land which the Lord thy God giveth thee.

"Thou shalt not kill.

"Thou shalt not commit adultery.

"Thou shalt not steal.

"Thou shalt not bear false witness against thy neighbour.

"Thou shalt not covet thy neighbour's house, thou shalt not covet thy neighbour's wife, nor his manservant, nor his maidservant, nor his ox, nor his ass, nor any thing that is thy neighbour's."

Sunday

The Lord summarized the Ten Commandments into two great commandments.

Matthew 22:37–39: "Jesus said unto him, Thou shalt love the Lord thy God with all thy heart, and with all thy soul, and with all thy mind.

"This is the first and great commandment.

"And the second is like unto it, Thou shalt love thy neighbour as thyself."

Quote

"One of Satan's most frequently used deceptions is the notion that the commandments of God are meant to restrict freedom and limit happiness."

—Ezra Taft Benson (former President of the Church)

Thoughtful Questions

- How can keeping the commandments bring us freedom, even happiness?
- What happens if we break a commandment?
- How will the Lord help us keep His commandments?

Supporting Conference Address

Robert D. Hales, "If Ye Love Me, Keep My Commandments," *Ensign*, May 2014.

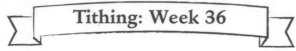

Tithing: Week 36

Daily Scripture Discussions

Monday

The Bible teaches us that even in ancient times, God's people followed the law of tithing. Abraham paid tithes.

Genesis 14:17–20: "And the king of Sodom went out to meet him after his return from the slaughter of Chedorlaomer, and of the kings that were with him, at the valley of Shaveh, which is the king's dale.

"And Melchizedek king of Salem brought forth bread and wine: and he was the priest of the most high God.

"And he blessed him, and said, Blessed be Abram of the most high God, possessor of heaven and earth:

"And blessed be the most high God, which hath delivered thine enemies into thy hand. And he gave him tithes of all."

Alma 13:15: "And it was this same Melchizedek to whom Abraham paid tithes; yea, even our father Abraham paid tithes of one-tenth part of all he possessed."

Tuesday

One-tenth of all we have belongs to the Lord.

Leviticus 27: 30–34: "And all the tithe of the land, whether of the seed of the land, or of the fruit of the tree, is the Lord's: it is holy unto the Lord.

"And if a man will at all redeem ought of his tithes, he shall add thereto the fifth part thereof.

"And concerning the tithe of the herd, or of the flock, even of whatsoever passeth under the rod, the tenth shall be holy unto the Lord.

"He shall not search whether it be good or bad, neither shall he change it: and if he change it at all, then both it and the change thereof shall be holy; it shall not be redeemed.

"These are the commandments, which the Lord commanded Moses for the children of Israel in mount Sinai."

Wednesday

In 1838, God revealed to the Prophet Joseph Smith the law of tithing and how much He requires His people to pay in tithes.

D&C 119:4–5: "And after that, those who have thus been tithed shall pay one-tenth of all their interest annually; and this shall be a standing law unto them forever, for my holy priesthood, saith the Lord.

"Verily I say unto you, it shall come to pass that all those who gather unto the land of Zion shall be tithed of their surplus properties, and shall observe this law, or they shall not be found worthy to abide among you."

Thursday

It is no surprise that when we keep the law of tithing, we receive great blessings from the Lord. These may not come in the way we expect, but they do come in His due time.

Malachi 3:10: "Bring ye all the tithes into the storehouse, that there may be meat in mine house, and prove me now herewith, saith the Lord of hosts, if I will not open you the windows of heaven, and pour you out a blessing, that there shall not be room enough to receive it."

D&C 64:23: "Behold, now it is called today until the coming of the Son of Man, and verily it is a day of sacrifice, and a day for the tithing of my people; for he that is tithed shall not be burned at his coming."

Friday

Where does our tithing money go?

D&C 120:1: "Verily, thus saith the Lord, the time is now come, that it shall be disposed of by a council, composed of the First Presidency of my Church, and of the bishop and his council; and by my high council; and by mine own voice unto them, saith the Lord. Even so. Amen."

D&C 97:11–12: "Yea, let it be built speedily, by the tithing of my people.

"Behold, this is the tithing and the sacrifice which I, the Lord, require at their hands, that there may be a house built unto me for the salvation of Zion."

Saturday

We learn from the story of the widow's mite how important it is to pay our tithing, even if it means we won't have much money left.

Mark 12:41–44: "And Jesus sat over against the treasury, and beheld how the people cast money into the treasury: and many that were rich cast in much.

"And there came a certain poor widow, and she threw in two mites, which make a farthing.

"And he called unto him his disciples, and saith unto them, Verily I say unto you, That this poor widow hath cast more in, than all they which have cast into the treasury:

"For all they did cast in of their abundance; but she of her want did cast in all that she had, even all her living."

Sunday

When we choose not to pay our tithing, we are robbing God of what He could use to build His church and robbing ourselves of the blessings we could receive.

Malachi 3: 8: "Will a man rob God? Yet ye have robbed me. But ye say, Wherein have we robbed thee? In tithes and offerings."

Quote

"Do you want the windows of heaven opened to you? Do you wish to receive blessings so great there is not room enough to receive them? Always pay your tithing and leave the outcome in the hands of the Lord."

—Joseph B. Wirthlin (member of the Quorum of the Twelve Apostles)

Thoughtful Questions

- Do you think it is easy or hard to pay your tithing?
- What are some things you can do to help you faithfully pay your tithing?
- Can you recognize any blessings from the Lord because you paid your tithing?

Supporting Conference Address

Robert D. Hales, "Tithing: A Test of Faith with Eternal Blessings," *Ensign*, November 2002.

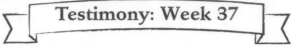

Testimony: Week 37

Daily Scripture Discussions

Monday

A testimony is what we believe to be true through a spiritual witness of the Holy Ghost.

Either 4:11: "But he that believeth these things which I have spoken, him will I visit with the manifestations of my Spirit, and he shall know and bear record. For because of my Spirit he shall know that these things are true; for it persuadeth men to do good."

Tuesday

The foundation of our testimonies as members of the Church is usually that our Heavenly Father lives, that He loves us, and that Jesus Christ lives, loves us, and atoned for our sins.

Job 19:25: "For I know that my redeemer liveth, and that he shall stand at the latter day upon the earth."

Jacob 4:4: "For, for this intent have we written these things, that they may know that we knew of Christ, and we had a hope of his glory many hundred years before his coming; and not only we ourselves had a hope of his glory, but also all the holy prophets which were before us."

Wednesday

You have the opportunity and responsibility to obtain your own testimony.

Alma 30:41: "But, behold, I have all things as a testimony that these things are true; and ye also have all things as a testimony unto you that they are true; and will ye deny them? Believest thou that these things are true?"

Thursday

With a sincere and righteous desire (and a little bit of faith), you can gain your own testimony. Alma taught this principle to a group of people who had yet to find their own testimony.

Alma 32:27: "But behold, if ye will awake and arouse your faculties, even to an experiment upon my words, and exercise a particle of faith, yea, even if ye can no more than desire to believe, let this desire work in you, even until ye believe in a manner that ye can give place for a portion of my words."

Friday

The gift of a testimony usually comes as a quiet assurance through the Holy Ghost—often after we make an effort to know such things.

Alma 5:45–46: "And this is not all. Do ye not suppose that I know of these things myself? Behold, I testify unto you that I do know that these things whereof I have spoken are true. And how do ye suppose that I know of their surety?

"Behold, I say unto you they are made known unto me by the Holy Spirit of God. Behold, I have fasted and prayed many days that I might know these things of myself. And now I do know of myself that they are true; for the Lord God hath made them manifest unto me by his Holy Spirit; and this is the spirit of revelation which is in me."

D&C 9:8: "But, behold, I say unto you, that you must study it out in your mind; then you must ask me if it be right, and if it is right I will cause that your bosom shall burn within you; therefore, you shall feel that it is right."

Saturday

Share your testimony! We are blessed—and we bless others—when we share our testimony.

D&C 62:3: "Nevertheless, ye are blessed, for the testimony which ye have borne is recorded in heaven for the angels to look upon; and they rejoice over you, and your sins are forgiven you."

D&C 84:62: "Therefore, go ye into all the world; and unto whatsoever place ye cannot go ye shall send, that the testimony may go from you into all the world unto every creature."

Sunday

As your testimony grows, Satan will try to overpower your testimony in different ways.

D&C 10:33: "Thus Satan thinketh to overpower your testimony in this generation, that the work may not come forth in this generation."

Quote

"Jesus teaches us another way: Go out. Go out and share your testimony, go out and interact with your brothers, go out and share, go out and ask. Become the Word in body as well as spirit."

—Pope Francis (leader of the Roman Catholic Church)

Thoughtful Questions

- What do you believe? What has the Spirit taught you to be true?
- What topic do you wish you had a stronger testimony about?
- Do you think it is hard to share your testimony?
- How might Satan try to overpower your testimony?

Supporting Conference Address

Dieter F. Uchtdorf, "The Power of a Personal Testimony," *Ensign*, November 2006.

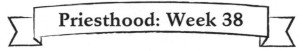

Priesthood: Week 38

Daily Scripture Discussions

Monday

Priesthood is the power and authority of God. It has always existed. Through it, God created and governs the heavens and the earth.

Alma 13:7–8: "This high priesthood being after the order of his Son, which order was from the foundation of the world; or in other words, being without beginning of days or end of years, being prepared from eternity to all eternity, according to his foreknowledge of all things—

"Now they were ordained after this manner—being called with a holy calling, and ordained with a holy ordinance, and taking upon them the high priesthood of the holy order, which calling, and ordinance, and high priesthood, is without beginning or end."

D&C 84:17–18: "Which priesthood continueth in the church of God in all generations, and is without beginning of days or end of years.

"And the Lord confirmed a priesthood also upon Aaron and his seed, throughout all their generations, which priesthood also continueth and abideth forever with the priesthood which is after the holiest order of God."

Tuesday

Following the death of Jesus and his Apostles, the earth experienced the dark ages, and the priesthood blessings and ordinances were withheld from those on earth. But the priesthood and its blessings were restored to Joseph Smith, beginning in 1820.

D&C 132:45: "For I have conferred upon you the keys and power of the priesthood, wherein I restore all things, and make known unto you all things in due time."

D&C 65:2: "The keys of the kingdom of God are committed unto man on the earth, and from thence shall the gospel roll forth unto the ends of the earth, as the stone which is cut out of the mountain without hands shall roll forth, until it has filled the whole earth."

D&C 124:123: "Verily I say unto you, I now give unto you the officers belonging to my Priesthood, that ye may hold the keys thereof, even the Priesthood which is after the order of Melchizedek, which is after the order of mine Only Begotten Son."

Wednesday

God gives priesthood authority to worthy male members of The Church of Jesus Christ of Latter-day Saints so they can act in His name.

D&C 42:11: "Again I say unto you, that it shall not be given to any one to go forth to preach my gospel, or to build up my church, except he be ordained by some one who has authority, and it is known to the church that he has authority and has been regularly ordained by the heads of the church."

Hebrews 5:4: "And no man taketh this honour unto himself, but he that is called of God, as was Aaron."

Thursday

The authority of the priesthood is given to worthy men through the laying on of hands upon their head by someone who is in authority.

Articles of Faith 1:5: "We believe that a man must be called of God, by prophecy, and by the laying on of hands by those who are in authority, to preach the Gospel and administer in the ordinances thereof."

Friday

It's important to know the blessings of the priesthood are available to *everyone*, not just men.

2 Nephi 26:33: "For none of these iniquities come of the Lord; for he doeth that which is good among the children of men; and he doeth nothing save it be plain unto the children of men; and he inviteth them all to come unto him and partake of his goodness; and he denieth none that come unto him, black and white, bond and free, male and female; and he remembereth the heathen; and all are alike unto God, both Jew and Gentile."

Saturday

The power of the priesthood is only available through righteousness and meekness—not pride, power, or unrighteous dominion.

D&C 121:36: "That the rights of the priesthood are inseparably connected with the powers of heaven, and that the powers of heaven cannot be controlled nor handled only upon the principles of righteousness."

D&C 121:41–43: "No power or influence can or ought to be maintained by virtue of the priesthood, only by persuasion, by long-suffering, by gentleness and meekness, and by love unfeigned;

"By kindness, and pure knowledge, which shall greatly enlarge the soul without hypocrisy, and without guile—

"Reproving betimes with sharpness, when moved upon by the Holy Ghost; and then showing forth afterwards an increase of love toward him whom thou hast reproved, lest he esteem thee to be his enemy."

Sunday

Another duty of priesthood holders is to look out for the members of the Church and their various needs.

D&C 20:53: "The teacher's duty is to watch over the church always, and be with and strengthen them."

Quote

"The greatest power God has given to His sons cannot be exercised without the companionship of one of His daughters, because only to His daughters has God given the power 'to be a creator of bodies . . . so that God's design and the Great Plan might meet fruition.' Those are the words of President J. Reuben Clark."

> —Dallin H. Oaks (member of the Quorum of the Twelve Apostles)

Thoughtful Questions

- What are some of the blessings of the priesthood?
- What are ways you can actively participate in the priesthood?

Supporting Conference Address

Robert D. Hales, "Blessings of the Priesthood," *Ensign*, November 1995.

Nicole Carpenter

Righteousness: Week 39

Daily Scripture Discussions

Monday

Righteousness is choosing good over evil and right over wrong.

2 Nephi 2:13: "And if ye shall say there is no law, ye shall also say there is no sin. If ye shall say there is no sin, ye shall also say there is no righteousness. And if there be no righteousness there be no happiness. And if there be no righteousness nor happiness there be no punishment nor misery. And if these things are not there is no God. And if there is no God we are not, neither the earth; for there could have been no creation of things, neither to act nor to be acted upon; wherefore, all things must have vanished away."

Ezekiel 18:20–21: "The soul that sinneth, it shall die. The son shall not bear the iniquity of the father, neither shall the father bear the iniquity of the son: the righteousness of the righteous shall be upon him, and the wickedness of the wicked shall be upon him.

"But if the wicked will turn from all his sins that he hath committed, and keep all my statutes, and do that which is lawful and right, he shall surely live, he shall not die."

Tuesday

We should seek after righteousness.

3 Nephi 13:33: "But seek ye first the kingdom of God and his righteousness, and all these things shall be added unto you."

Matthew 5:6: "Blessed are they which do hunger and thirst after righteousness: for they shall be filled."

Wednesday

The Lord watches over and protects his righteous disciples.

Psalm 34: 15, 17: "The eyes of the Lord are upon the righteous, and his ears are open unto their cry.

"The righteous cry, and the Lord heareth, and delivereth them out of all their troubles."

Thursday

Righteousness brings peace.

Isaiah 32:17: "And the work of righteousness shall be peace; and the effect of righteousness quietness and assurance for ever."

Friday

Righteousness brings happiness.

Mosiah 2:41: "And moreover, I would desire that ye should consider on the blessed and happy state of those that keep the commandments of God. For behold, they are blessed in all things, both temporal and spiritual; and if they hold out faithful to the end they are received into heaven, that thereby they may dwell with God in a state of never-ending happiness. O remember, remember that these things are true; for the Lord God hath spoken it."

1 Peter 3:14: "But and if ye suffer for righteousness' sake, happy are ye: and be not afraid of their terror, neither be troubled."

Saturday

We can be examples of goodness.

D&C 58:27–29: "Verily I say, men should be anxiously engaged in a good cause, and do many things of their own free will, and bring to pass much righteousness;

"For the power is in them, wherein they are agents unto themselves. And inasmuch as men do good they shall in nowise lose their reward.

"But he that doeth not anything until he is commanded, and receiveth a commandment with doubtful heart, and keepeth it with slothfulness, the same is damned."

Sunday

When we need to judge others, it's important to judge them righteously.

Leviticus 19:15: "Ye shall do no unrighteousness in judgment: thou shalt not respect the person of the poor, nor honour the person of the mighty: but in righteousness shalt thou judge thy neighbour."

Quote

"True religion is real living; living with all one's soul, with all one's goodness and righteousness."

—Albert Einstein (theoretical physicist)

Thoughtful Questions

- What is self-righteousness (moral superiority)? How is it different from being righteous?
- What can you do to spread righteousness?
- How does it make you feel when you choose good things? Bad things?

Supporting Conference Address

William R. Bradford, "Righteousness," *Ensign*, November 1999.

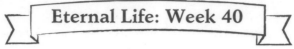

Eternal Life: Week 40

Daily Scripture Discussions

Monday

Eternal life is the greatest gift we have been given.

D&C 14:7: "And, if you keep my commandments and endure to the end you shall have eternal life, which gift is the greatest of all the gifts of God."

Tuesday

The gift of eternal life comes through the Atonement of our Savior Jesus Christ.

John 3:16: "For God so loved the world, that he gave his only begotten Son, that whosoever believeth in him should not perish, but have everlasting life."

Wednesday

We should work to personally know our Savior and feel His love in our lives.

John 17:3: "And this is life eternal, that they might know thee the only true God, and Jesus Christ, whom thou hast sent."

Thursday

When we are baptized and receive the gift of the Holy Ghost, we begin the path that leads to eternal life.

2 Nephi 31:17–18: "The gate by which ye should enter is repentance and baptism by water; and then cometh a remission of your sins by fire and by the Holy Ghost.

"And then are ye in this strait and narrow path which leads to eternal life; yea, ye have entered in by the gate; ye have done according to the commandments of the Father and the Son; and ye have received the Holy Ghost, which witnesses of the Father and the Son, unto the fulfilling of the promise which he hath made, that if ye entered in by the way ye should receive."

Friday

After baptism, we must continue to press forward and keep commandments that keep us on the path to eternal life.

2 Nephi 31:19–20: "And now, my beloved brethren, after ye have gotten into this strait and narrow path, I would ask if all is done? Behold, I say unto you, Nay; for ye have not come thus far save it were by the word of Christ with unshaken faith in him, relying wholly upon the merits of him who is mighty to save.

"Wherefore, ye must press forward with a steadfastness in Christ, having a perfect brightness of hope, and a love of God and of all men. Wherefore, if ye shall press forward, feasting upon the word of Christ, and endure to the end, behold, thus saith the Father: Ye shall have eternal life."

Saturday

To have eternal life is to inherit a place in the highest degree in the celestial kingdom in heaven. Here we will live in God's presence and continue as families.

D&C 131:1–4: "In the celestial glory there are three heavens or degrees;

"And in order to obtain the highest, a man must enter into this order of the priesthood [meaning the new and everlasting covenant of marriage];

"And if he does not, he cannot obtain it.

"He may enter into the other, but that is the end of his kingdom; he cannot have an increase."

Sunday

We don't need to be perfect to receive eternal life; we only need to do the best we can and use the Atonement, and then the Savior will take care of the rest.

2 Nephi 25:23: "For we labor diligently to write, to persuade our children, and also our brethren, to believe in Christ, and to be reconciled to God; for we know that it is by grace that we are saved, after all we can do."

Moroni 7:41: "And what is it that ye shall hope for? Behold I say unto you that ye shall have hope through the atonement of Christ and the power of his resurrection, to be raised unto life eternal, and this because of your faith in him according to the promise."

Quote

"No one who strives with full faith and heart for the blessings of eternal life will be denied. And how great will be the joy and how much deeper the appreciation then after enduring in patience and faith now."

—Henry B. Eyring (member of the First Presidency)

Thoughtful Questions

- What future do you want for yourself?
- What choices do you think are important to make to stay on the path of eternal life?
- How can you help others to stay on this same path?

Supporting Conference Address

Randall K. Bennett, "Choose Eternal Life," *Ensign*, November 2011.

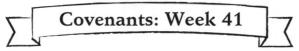

Covenants: Week 41

Daily Scripture Discussions

Monday

A covenant is an agreement between God and a person or group of people. God specifies the terms of the covenant.

2 Chronicles 15:12: "And they entered into a covenant to seek the Lord God of their fathers with all their heart and with all their soul."

Enos 1:16: "And I had faith, and I did cry unto God that he would preserve the records; and he covenanted with me that he would bring them forth unto the Lamanites in his own due time."

Tuesday

God keeps His covenants.

Deuteronomy 7:9: "Know therefore that the Lord thy God, he is God, the faithful God, which keepeth covenant and mercy with them that love him and keep his commandments to a thousand generations."

2 Nephi 6:12: "And blessed are the Gentiles, they of whom the prophet has written; for behold, if it so be that they shall repent and fight not against Zion, and do not unite themselves to that great and abominable church, they shall be saved; for the Lord God will fulfil his covenants which he has made unto his children; and for this cause the prophet has written these things."

Wednesday

We receive blessings when we keep our covenants. And likewise, we miss promises and blessings when we don't keep our covenants.

D&C 82:10: "I, the Lord, am bound when ye do what I say; but when ye do not what I say, ye have no promise."

D&C 54:6: "But blessed are they who have kept the covenant and observed the commandment, for they shall obtain mercy.

Thursday

Covenants often require faith and sacrifice on our part.

D&C 97:8: "Verily I say unto you, all among them who know their hearts are honest, and are broken, and their spirits contrite, and are willing to observe their covenants by sacrifice—yea, every sacrifice which I, the Lord, shall command—they are accepted of me."

Psalm 50:5: "Gather my saints together unto me; those that have made a covenant with me by sacrifice."

Friday

Remember and honor your covenants, and you won't need to be commanded in everything you do.

D&C 58:26–29: "For behold, it is not meet that I should command in all things; for he that is compelled in all things, the same is a slothful and not a wise servant; wherefore he receiveth no reward.

"Verily I say, men should be anxiously engaged in a good cause, and do many things of their own free will, and bring to pass much righteousness;

"For the power is in them, wherein they are agents unto themselves. And inasmuch as men do good they shall in nowise lose their reward.

"But he that doeth not anything until he is commanded, and receiveth a commandment with doubtful heart, and keepeth it with slothfulness, the same is damned."

Saturday

After the earth flooded, the Lord covenanted with Noah and left us a rainbow as a reminder of that covenant.

Genesis 9:14–16: "And it shall come to pass, when I bring a cloud over the earth, that the bow shall be seen in the cloud:

"And I will remember my covenant, which is between me and you and every living creature of all flesh; and the waters shall no more become a flood to destroy all flesh.

"And the bow shall be in the cloud; and I will look upon it, that I may remember the everlasting covenant between God and every living creature of all flesh that is upon the earth."

Sunday

When we are baptized, we make covenants with the Lord that we can renew each week through partaking of the sacrament.

Mosiah 18:8–10: "And it came to pass that he said unto them: Behold, here are the waters of Mormon (for thus were they called) and now, as ye are desirous to come into the fold of God, and to be called his people, and are willing to bear one another's burdens, that they may be light;

"Yea, and are willing to mourn with those that mourn; yea, and comfort those that stand in need of comfort, and to stand as witnesses of God at all times and in all things, and in all places that ye may be in, even until death, that ye may be redeemed of God, and be numbered with those of the first resurrection, that ye may have eternal life—

"Now I say unto you, if this be the desire of your hearts, what have you against being baptized in the name of the Lord, as a witness before him that ye have entered into a covenant with him, that ye will serve him and keep his commandments, that he may pour out his Spirit more abundantly upon you?"

Quote

"A covenant made with God should be regarded not as restrictive but as protective."
　　　　　　　—Russell M. Nelson (member of the Quorum of the Twelve Apostles)

Thoughtful Questions

- How is a covenant stronger than a promise?
- If we choose to not keep our covenants, what are we also choosing?
- Next time you see a rainbow, what will you think?

Supporting Conference Address

Linda K. Burton, "The Power, Joy, and Love of Covenant Keeping," *Ensign*, November 2013.

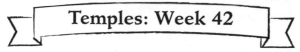

Temples: Week 42

Daily Scripture Discussions

Monday

Throughout history, the Lord has commanded His people to build temples. The temple is the Lord's house on earth.

2 Samuel 7:5–7: "Go and tell my servant David, Thus saith the Lord, Shalt thou build me an house for me to dwell in?

"Whereas I have not dwelt in any house since the time that I brought up the children of Israel out of Egypt, even to this day, but have walked in a tent and in a tabernacle.

"In all the places wherein I have walked with all the children of Israel spake I a word with any of the tribes of Israel, whom I commanded to feed my people Israel, saying, Why build ye not me an house of cedar?"

1 Kings 9:1–3: "And it came to pass, when Solomon had finished the building of the house of the Lord, and the king's house, and all Solomon's desire which he was pleased to do,

"That the Lord appeared to Solomon the second time, as he had appeared unto him at Gibeon.

"And the Lord said unto him, I have heard thy prayer and thy supplication, that thou hast made before me: I have hallowed this house, which thou hast built, to put my name there for ever; and mine eyes and mine heart shall be there perpetually."

Tuesday

The first temple to be built in this dispensation was the temple at Kirtland, Ohio. The Saints at the time were very poor, yet they obeyed the Lord's commandment and built it anyway.

D&C 88:119: "Organize yourselves; prepare every needful thing; and establish a house, even a house of prayer, a house of fasting, a house of faith, a house of learning, a house of glory, a house of order, a house of God."

D&C 109:5: "For thou knowest that we have done this work through great tribulation; and out of our poverty we have given of our substance to build a house to thy name, that the Son of Man might have a place to manifest himself to his people."

Wednesday

Temples are dedicated to and accepted by the Lord.

D&C 110:7–8: "For behold, I have accepted this house, and my name shall be here; and I will manifest myself to my people in mercy in this house.

"Yea, I will appear unto my servants, and speak unto them with mine own voice, if my people will keep my commandments, and do not pollute this holy house."

Thursday

Temples are a place of worship and learning.

Isaiah 2:2–3: "And it shall come to pass in the last days, that the mountain of the Lord's house shall be established in the top of the mountains, and shall be exalted above the hills; and all nations shall flow unto it.

"And many people shall go and say, Come ye, and let us go up to the mountain of the Lord, to the house of the God of Jacob; and he will teach us of his ways, and we will walk in his paths: for out of Zion shall go forth the law, and the word of the Lord from Jerusalem."

Friday

The temple is a place for sacred, saving ordinances and covenants.

D&C 128:13: "Consequently, the baptismal font was instituted as a similitude of the grave, and was commanded to be in a place underneath where the living are wont to assemble, to show forth the living and the dead, and that all things may have their likeness, and that they may accord one with another—that which is earthly conforming to that which is heavenly, as Paul hath declared, 1 Corinthians 15:46, 47, and 48."

D&C 138:54: "Including the building of the temples and the performance of ordinances therein for the redemption of the dead, were also in the spirit world."

D&C 138:48: "Foreshadowing the great work to be done in the temples of the Lord in the dispensation of the fulness of times, for the redemption of the dead, and the sealing of the children to their parents, lest the whole earth be smitten with a curse and utterly wasted at his coming."

Saturday

Only those who are worthy can enter the house of the Lord.

Alma 7:21: "And he doth not dwell in unholy temples; neither can filthiness or anything which is unclean be received into the kingdom of God; therefore I say unto you the time shall come, yea, and it shall be at the last day, that he who is filthy shall remain in his filthiness."

Sunday

Your body is a temple of God, so the Spirit of the Lord will withdraw from you if needed.

1 Corinthians 3:16: "Know ye not that ye are the temple of God, and that the Spirit of God dwelleth in you?"

1 Corinthians 6:19: "What? know ye not that your body is the temple of the Holy Ghost which is in you, which ye have of God, and ye are not your own?"

Helaman 4:24: "And they saw that they had become weak, like unto their brethren, the Lamanites, and that the Spirit of the Lord did no more preserve them; yea, it had withdrawn from them because the Spirit of the Lord doth not dwell in unholy temples."

Quote

"In addition to temples, surely another holy place on earth ought to be our homes. The feelings of holiness in my home prepared me for feelings of holiness in the temple."

—James E. Faust (former member of the First Presidency)

Thoughtful Questions

- Why do you think temples are important to the Lord? Why do we need so many?
- What is the difference between secret and sacred? Is the temple a secret or sacred place?
- How can you treat your body like a temple?
- How can we make our home a special place like the temple?

Supporting Conference Address

Carol B. Thomas, "Preparing Our Families for the Temple," *Ensign*, May 1999.

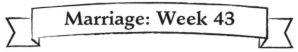

Marriage: Week 43

Daily Scripture Discussions

Monday

Marriage between a man and a woman is ordained of God.

D&C 49:15: "And again, verily I say unto you, that whoso forbiddeth to marry is not ordained of God, for marriage is ordained of God unto man."

Mark 10:6–8: "But from the beginning of the creation God made them male and female.

"For this cause shall a man leave his father and mother, and cleave to his wife;

"And they twain shall be one flesh: so then they are no more twain, but one flesh."

Tuesday

Couples who are married in the temple are sealed together as a family for all eternity.

D&C 132:19: "And again, verily I say unto you, if a man marry a wife by my word, which is my law, and by the new and everlasting covenant, and it is sealed unto them by the Holy Spirit of promise, by him who is anointed, unto whom I have appointed this power and the keys of this priesthood; . . . and if ye abide in my covenant, . . . it shall be done unto them in all things whatsoever my servant hath put upon them, in time, and through all eternity; and shall be of full force when they are out of the world; and they shall pass by the angels, and the gods, which are set there, to their exaltation and glory in all things, as hath been sealed upon their heads, which glory shall be a fulness and a continuation of the seeds forever and ever."

D&C 131:1–4: "In the celestial glory there are three heavens or degrees;

"And in order to obtain the highest, a man must enter into this order of the priesthood [meaning the new and everlasting covenant of marriage];

"And if he does not, he cannot obtain it.

"He may enter into the other, but that is the end of his kingdom; he cannot have an increase."

Wednesday

A husband should be loyal to his wife and love her beyond all else.

D&C 42:22: "Thou shalt love thy wife with all thy heart, and shalt cleave unto her and none else."

Ephesians 5:25: "Husbands, love your wives, even as Christ also loved the church, and gave himself for it."

Thursday

A wife should love her husband and delight in him.

Ephesians 5:22: "Wives, submit yourselves unto your own husbands, as unto the Lord."

D&C 25:13–14: "Wherefore, lift up thy heart and rejoice, and cleave unto the covenants which thou hast made.

"Continue in the spirit of meekness, and beware of pride. Let thy soul delight in thy husband, and the glory which shall come upon him."

Friday

A husband and wife should be faithful to each other.

1 Corinthians 7:2–3: "Nevertheless, to avoid fornication, let every man have his own wife, and let every woman have her own husband.

"Let the husband render unto the wife due benevolence: and likewise also the wife unto the husband."

Saturday

You can set a goal and prepare now for a celestial marriage.

Alma 37:35: "O, remember, my son, and learn wisdom in thy youth; yea, learn in thy youth to keep the commandments of God."

Sunday

Even for the faithful, marriage doesn't always work out like we had hoped. And for some, marriage is never an option. The Lord promises to work these things out and bless you.

Romans 8:28: "And we know that all things work together for good to them that love God, to them who are the called according to his purpose."

Quote

"A successful marriage requires falling in love many times and always with the same person."

—Mignon McLaughlin (journalist)

Thoughtful Questions

- Why is marriage between a man and woman so important?
- Why does Heavenly Father want his sons and daughters to get married in the temple?
- How would you want to treat your future spouse?
- What things can we do now to prepare for celestial marriage?

Supporting Conference Address

L. Whitney Clayton, "Marriage: Watch and Learn," *Ensign*, May 2013.

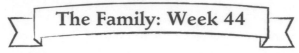

The Family: Week 44

Daily Scripture Discussions

Monday

We come from a heavenly family and are sons and daughters of our Heavenly Father.
1 Nephi 17:36: "Behold, the Lord hath created the earth that it should be inhabited; and he hath created his children that they should possess it."

Tuesday

The creation of the world was completed with the creation of the family.
Genesis 2:15, 18, 22: "And the Lord God took the man, and put him into the garden of Eden to dress it and to keep it.

"And the Lord God said, It is not good that the man should be alone; I will make him an help meet for him.

"And the rib, which the Lord God had taken from man, made he a woman, and brought her unto the man."

Moses 5:12: "And Adam and Eve blessed the name of God, and they made all things known unto their sons and their daughters."

Wednesday

Parents are to love and teach their children.
D&C 93:40: "But I have commanded you to bring up your children in light and truth."

Proverbs 22:6: "Train up a child in the way he should go: and when he is old, he will not depart from it."

Mosiah 4:15: "But ye will teach them to walk in the ways of truth and soberness; ye will teach them to love one another, and to serve one another."

Thursday

Children are to honor and obey their parents.

Exodus 20:12: "Honour thy father and thy mother: that thy days may be long upon the land which the Lord thy God giveth thee."

Colossians 3:20: "Children, obey your parents in all things: for this is well pleasing unto the Lord."

Friday

Families should worship together.

3 Nephi 18:21: "Pray in your families unto the Father, always in my name, that your wives and your children may be blessed."

2 Nephi 25:26: "And we talk of Christ, we rejoice in Christ, we preach of Christ, we prophesy of Christ, and we write according to our prophecies, that our children may know to what source they may look for a remission of their sins."

Saturday

Help create a home of love and peace for your family.

1 John 2:10: "He that loveth his brother abideth in the light, and there is none occasion of stumbling in him."

Proverbs 15:1: "A soft answer turneth away wrath: but grievous words stir up anger."

3 Nephi 11:29: "For verily, verily I say unto you, he that hath the spirit of contention is not of me, but is of the devil, who is the father of contention, and he stirreth up the hearts of men to contend with anger, one with another."

Colossians 3:21: "Fathers, provoke not your children to anger, lest they be discouraged."

Sunday

The family unit is an eternal principle and will continue to exist in heaven.

D&C 130:1–2: "When the Savior shall appear we shall see him as he is. We shall see that he is a man like ourselves.

"And that same sociality which exists among us here will exist among us there, only it will be coupled with eternal glory, which glory we do not now enjoy."

Additional Reading

For additional reading, see "The Family: A Proclamation to the World."

Quote

"Family is not an important thing. It's everything."

—Michael J. Fox (actor)

Thoughtful Questions

- In what way do you know you are a child of God?
- Why is it important for us to respect each other?
- Why is it easier for us to be nice to strangers and friends than it is to be nice to family members?
- What can we do to feel more love in our home?

Supporting Conference Address

Mary N. Cook, "Strengthen Home and Family," *Ensign*, November 2007.

Spiritual Gifts: Week 45

Daily Scripture Discussions

Monday

Spiritual gifts are gifts from God through the Holy Ghost.

James 1:17: "Every good gift and every perfect gift is from above, and cometh down from the Father of lights, with whom is no variableness, neither shadow of turning."

D&C 6:10: "Behold thou hast a gift, and blessed art thou because of thy gift. Remember it is sacred and cometh from above."

Tuesday

God gives at least one spiritual gift to every faithful person who has received the gift of the Holy Ghost.

D&C 46:11–12: "For all have not every gift given unto them; for there are many gifts, and to every man is given a gift by the Spirit of God.

"To some is given one, and to some is given another, that all may be profited thereby."

Moroni 10:17: "And all these gifts come by the Spirit of Christ; and they come unto every man severally, according as he will."

Wednesday

The Lord encourages us to earnestly seek for other spiritual gifts.

D&C 46:8: "Wherefore, beware lest ye are deceived; and that ye may not be deceived seek ye earnestly the best gifts, always remembering for what they are given."

Thursday

As you receive these gifts, they will strengthen you and help you to bless and strengthen others.

D&C 46:26: "And all these gifts come from God, for the benefit of the children of God."

D&C 46:9: "For verily I say unto you, they are given for the benefit of those who love me and keep all my commandments, and him that seeketh so to do; that all may be benefited that seek or that ask of me, that ask and not for a sign that they may consume it upon their lusts."

Friday

We learn many examples of spiritual gifts from the scriptures. (See also 1 Corinthians 12:8–10, D&C 46:13–25.)

Moroni 10:8–16: "And again, I exhort you, my brethren, that ye deny not the gifts of God, for they are many; and they come from the same God. And there are different ways that these gifts are administered; but it is the same God who worketh all in all; and they are given by the manifestations of the Spirit of God unto men, to profit them.

"For behold, to one is given by the Spirit of God, that he may teach the word of wisdom;

"And to another, that he may teach the word of knowledge by the same Spirit;

"And to another, exceedingly great faith; and to another, the gifts of healing by the same Spirit;

"And again, to another, that he may work mighty miracles;

"And again, to another, that he may prophesy concerning all things;

"And again, to another, the beholding of angels and ministering spirits;

"And again, to another, all kinds of tongues;

"And again, to another, the interpretation of languages and of divers kinds of tongues."

Saturday

Don't neglect your spiritual gifts.

1 Timothy 4:14: "Neglect not the gift that is in thee, which was given thee by prophecy, with the laying on of the hands of the presbytery."

Sunday

Spiritual gifts may seem special, but above all else, charity is most important.

1 Corinthians 13:1–2: "Though I speak with the tongues of men and of angels, and have not charity, I am become as sounding brass, or a tinkling cymbal.

"And though I have the gift of prophecy, and understand all mysteries, and all knowledge; and though I have all faith, so that I could remove mountains, and have not charity, I am nothing."

Quote

"It's one of the greatest gifts you can give yourself, to forgive. Forgive everybody."

—Maya Angelou (author)

Thoughtful Questions

- What is the difference between the Light of Christ and the Holy Ghost?
- How can the Holy Ghost show us our spiritual gift(s)?
- Can you think of a spiritual gift you have?
- Can you think of any instances in which you would seek another spiritual gift?

Supporting Conference Address

Robert D. Hales, "Gifts of the Spirit," *Ensign*, February 2002.

Holiday Lessons

Love and Valentine's Day: Week 46

Daily Scripture Discussions

Monday

God is love.

1 John 4:16: "And we have known and believed the love that God hath to us. God is love; and he that dwelleth in love dwelleth in God, and God in him."

Tuesday

God loved us so much He sacrificed His Son that we might have a Savior and return to live with Him.

John 3:16: "For God so loved the world, that he gave his only begotten Son, that whosoever believeth in him should not perish, but have everlasting life."

Wednesday

We get to choose if we want to love God with our whole heart.

Deuteronomy 13:3: "Thou shalt not hearken unto the words of that prophet, or that dreamer of dreams: for the Lord your God proveth you, to know whether ye love the Lord your God with all your heart and with all your soul."

Thursday

We show our love for God by keeping His commandments and serving His children.

D&C 59:5: "Wherefore, I give unto them a commandment, saying thus: Thou shalt love the Lord thy God with all thy heart, with all thy might, mind, and strength; and in the name of Jesus Christ thou shalt serve him."

John 14:15: "If ye love me, keep my commandments."

Friday

Before we can love others, we must first learn to love ourselves.

Mark 12:31: "And the second is like, namely this, Thou shalt love thy neighbour as thyself. There is none other commandment greater than these."

Saturday

It's important to love one another as God loves us.

John 13:34: "A new commandment I give unto you, That ye love one another; as I have loved you, that ye also love one another."

1 John 4:12: "No man hath seen God at any time. If we love one another, God dwelleth in us, and his love is perfected in us."

Sunday

We can even learn to love our enemies.

Matthew 5:44: "But I say unto you, Love your enemies, bless them that curse you, do good to them that hate you, and pray for them which despitefully use you, and persecute you."

Quote

"Let us always meet each other with smile, for the smile is the beginning of love."

—Mother Teresa (founder of Missionaries of Charity)

Thoughtful Questions

- When do you feel loved?
- When you look in the mirror, do you feel love?
- How have you "proven" your love for God?
- Who is your "neighbor" you are supposed to love?

Supporting Conference Address

Thomas S. Monson, "Love—the Essence of the Gospel," *Ensign*, May 2014.

The Atonement of Jesus Christ and Easter (Part 1): Week 47

Daily Scripture Discussions

Monday

In the Garden of Gethsemane, the Savior submitted to the Father's will and began to suffer for the afflictions and sins of all of us. Christ was afterward betrayed.

Luke 22:41–45: "And he was withdrawn from them about a stone's cast, and kneeled down, and prayed,

"Saying, Father, if thou be willing, remove this cup from me: nevertheless not my will, but thine, be done.

"And there appeared an angel unto him from heaven, strengthening him.

"And being in an agony he prayed more earnestly: and his sweat was as it were great drops of blood falling down to the ground.

"And when he rose up from prayer, and was come to his disciples, he found them sleeping for sorrow."

Matthew 26:36–54: "Then cometh Jesus with them unto a place called Gethsemane, and saith unto the disciples, Sit ye here, while I go and pray yonder.

"And he took with him Peter and the two sons of Zebedee, and began to be sorrowful and very heavy.

"Then saith he unto them, My soul is exceeding sorrowful, even unto death: tarry ye here, and watch with me.

"And he went a little further, and fell on his face, and prayed, saying, O my Father, if it be possible, let this cup pass from me: nevertheless not as I will, but as thou wilt.

"And he cometh unto the disciples, and findeth them asleep, and saith unto Peter, What, could ye not watch with me one hour?

"Watch and pray, that ye enter not into temptation: the spirit indeed is willing, but the flesh is weak.

"He went away again the second time, and prayed, saying, O my Father, if this cup may not pass away from me, except I drink it, thy will be done.

"And he came and found them asleep again: for their eyes were heavy.

"And he left them, and went away again, and prayed the third time, saying the same words.

"Then cometh he to his disciples, and saith unto them, Sleep on now, and take your rest: behold, the hour is at hand, and the Son of man is betrayed into the hands of sinners.

"Rise, let us be going: behold, he is at hand that doth betray me.

"And while he yet spake, lo, Judas, one of the twelve, came, and with him a great multitude with swords and staves, from the chief priests and elders of the people.

"Now he that betrayed him gave them a sign, saying, Whomsoever I shall kiss, that same is he: hold him fast.

"And forthwith he came to Jesus, and said, Hail, master; and kissed him.

"And Jesus said unto him, Friend, wherefore art thou come? Then came they, and laid hands on Jesus, and took him.

"And, behold, one of them which were with Jesus stretched out his hand, and drew his sword, and struck a servant of the high priest's, and smote off his ear.

"Then said Jesus unto him, Put up again thy sword into his place: for all they that take the sword shall perish with the sword.

"Thinkest thou that I cannot now pray to my Father, and he shall presently give me more than twelve legions of angels?

"But how then shall the scriptures be fulfilled, that thus it must be?"

Tuesday

Jesus was taken to Pontius Pilate, the governor.

John 18:33–38: "Then Pilate entered into the judgment hall again, and called Jesus, and said unto him, Art thou the King of the Jews?

"Jesus answered him, Sayest thou this thing of thyself, or did others tell it thee of me?

"Pilate answered, Am I a Jew? Thine own nation and the chief priests have delivered thee unto me: what hast thou done?

"Jesus answered, My kingdom is not of this world: if my kingdom were of this world, then would my servants fight, that I should not be delivered to the Jews: but now is my kingdom not from hence.

"Pilate therefore said unto him, Art thou a king then? Jesus answered, Thou sayest that I am a king. To this end was I born, and for this cause came I into the world, that I should bear witness unto the truth. Every one that is of the truth heareth my voice.

"Pilate saith unto him, What is truth? And when he had said this, he went out again unto the Jews, and saith unto them, I find in him no fault at all."

Wednesday

Pilate thought Jesus was innocent but sentenced him to death anyway.

Luke 23:13–24: "And Pilate, when he had called together the chief priests and the rulers and the people,

"Said unto them, Ye have brought this man unto me, as one that perverteth the people: and, behold, I, having examined him before you, have found no fault in this man touching those things whereof ye accuse him:

"No, nor yet Herod: for I sent you to him; and, lo, nothing worthy of death is done unto him.

"I will therefore chastise him, and release him.

"(For of necessity he must release one unto them at the feast.)

"And they cried out all at once, saying, Away with this man, and release unto us Barabbas:

"(Who for a certain sedition made in the city, and for murder, was cast into prison.)

"Pilate therefore, willing to release Jesus, spake again to them.

"But they cried, saying, Crucify him, crucify him.

"And he said unto them the third time, Why, what evil hath he done? I have found no cause of death in him: I will therefore chastise him, and let him go.

"And they were instant with loud voices, requiring that he might be crucified. And the voices of them and of the chief priests prevailed.

"And Pilate gave sentence that it should be as they required."

Matthew 27:24–26: "When Pilate saw that he could prevail nothing, but that rather a tumult was made, he took water, and washed his hands before the multitude, saying, I am innocent of the blood of this just person: see ye to it.

"Then answered all the people, and said, His blood be on us, and on our children.

"Then released he Barabbas unto them: and when he had scourged Jesus, he delivered him to be crucified."

Thursday

Soldiers mocked Jesus. They took Him to Calvary and nailed Him to a cross.

Matthew 27:27–31: "Then the soldiers of the governor took Jesus into the common hall, and gathered unto him the whole band of soldiers.

"And they stripped him, and put on him a scarlet robe.

"And when they had plaited a crown of thorns, they put it upon his head, and a reed in his right hand: and they bowed the knee before him, and mocked him, saying, Hail, King of the Jews!

"And they spit upon him, and took the reed, and smote him on the head.

"And after that they had mocked him, they took the robe off from him, and put his own raiment on him, and led him away to crucify him."

John 19:16–19: "Then delivered he him therefore unto them to be crucified. And they took Jesus, and led him away.

"And he bearing his cross went forth into a place called the place of a skull, which is called in the Hebrew Golgotha:

"Where they crucified him, and two other with him, on either side one, and Jesus in the midst.

"And Pilate wrote a title, and put it on the cross. And the writing was, Jesus of Nazareth the King of the Jews."

Friday

Jesus asked for God to forgive the people who condemned Him and the soldiers who crucified Him. Christ then had a conversation with the prisoners.

Luke 23:32–34, 39–44: "And there were also two other, malefactors, led with him to be put to death.

"And when they were come to the place, which is called Calvary, there they crucified him, and the malefactors, one on the right hand, and the other on the left.

"Then said Jesus, Father, forgive them; for they know not what they do. And they parted his raiment, and cast lots.

"And one of the malefactors which were hanged railed on him, saying, If thou be Christ, save thyself and us.

"But the other answering rebuked him, saying, Dost not thou fear God, seeing thou art in the same condemnation?

"And we indeed justly; for we receive the due reward of our deeds: but this man hath done nothing amiss.

"And he said unto Jesus, Lord, remember me when thou comest into thy kingdom.

"And Jesus said unto him, Verily I say unto thee, To day shalt thou be with me in paradise.

"And it was about the sixth hour, and there was a darkness over all the earth until the ninth hour."

Saturday

Jesus ensured His mother Mary was taken care of. He surrendered His spirit and died.

John 19:25–27: "Now there stood by the cross of Jesus his mother, and his mother's sister, Mary the wife of Cleophas, and Mary Magdalene.

"When Jesus therefore saw his mother, and the disciple standing by, whom he loved, he saith unto his mother, Woman, behold thy son!

"Then saith he to the disciple, Behold thy mother! And from that hour that disciple took her unto his own home."

Matthew 27:46, 50–51: "And about the ninth hour Jesus cried with a loud voice, saying, Eli, Eli, lama sabachthani? that is to say, My God, my God, why hast thou forsaken me?

"Jesus, when he had cried again with a loud voice, yielded up the ghost.

"And, behold, the veil of the temple was rent in twain from the top to the bottom; and the earth did quake, and the rocks rent."

Luke 23:46: "And when Jesus had cried with a loud voice, he said, Father, into thy hands I commend my spirit: and having said thus, he gave up the ghost."

Sunday

Not a single bone of Jesus Christ was broken.

John 19:31–36: "The Jews therefore, because it was the preparation, that the bodies should not remain upon the cross on the sabbath day, (for that sabbath day was an high day,) besought Pilate that their legs might be broken, and that they might be taken away.

"Then came the soldiers, and brake the legs of the first, and of the other which was crucified with him.

"But when they came to Jesus, and saw that he was dead already, they brake not his legs:

"But one of the soldiers with a spear pierced his side, and forthwith came there out blood and water.

"And he that saw it bare record, and his record is true: and he knoweth that he saith true, that ye might believe.

"For these things were done, that the scripture should be fulfilled, A bone of him shall not be broken."

Quote

"By the power of the Atonement, people I know well and love became new, and the effects of sin were wiped away. My heart has been filled with love for the Savior and the loving Father who sent Him."

—Henry B. Eyring (member of the First Presidency)

Thoughtful Questions

- What does the Atonement mean to you?
- Why was it important for a perfect person to suffer and feel so much pain?
- How can we use the Atonement each day in our individual lives?

Supporting Conference Address

Carlos H. Amado, "Christ the Redeemer," *Ensign*, May 2014.

Supporting Videos

"The Savior Suffers in Gethsemane," "My Kingdom Is Not of This World," "Jesus Is Scourged and Crucified," and "None Were with Him—An Apostle's Easter Thoughts on Christ"; available at lds.org/media-library.

The Resurrection of Jesus Christ and Easter (Part 2): Week 48

Daily Scripture Discussions

Monday

Jesus's body was taken and placed in a sepulchre.

Matthew 27:57–60: "When the even was come, there came a rich man of Arimathaea, named Joseph, who also himself was Jesus' disciple:

"He went to Pilate, and begged the body of Jesus. Then Pilate commanded the body to be delivered.

"And when Joseph had taken the body, he wrapped it in a clean linen cloth,

"And laid it in his own new tomb, which he had hewn out in the rock: and he rolled a great stone to the door of the sepulchre, and departed."

Tuesday

Women came to the tomb to anoint the body of Christ and discovered angels had moved the stone and rendered the guards unconscious.

Matthew 28:1–6: "In the end of the sabbath, as it began to dawn toward the first day of the week, came Mary Magdalene and the other Mary to see the sepulchre.

"And, behold, there was a great earthquake: for the angel of the Lord descended from heaven, and came and rolled back the stone from the door, and sat upon it.

"His countenance was like lightning, and his raiment white as snow:

"And for fear of him the keepers did shake, and became as dead men.

"And the angel answered and said unto the women, Fear not ye: for I know that ye seek Jesus, which was crucified.

"He is not here: for he is risen, as he said. Come, see the place where the Lord lay."

Luke 24:1–4: "Now upon the first day of the week, very early in the morning, they came unto the sepulchre, bringing the spices which they had prepared, and certain others with them.

"And they found the stone rolled away from the sepulchre.

"And they entered in, and found not the body of the Lord Jesus.

"And it came to pass, as they were much perplexed thereabout, behold, two men stood by them in shining garments."

Wednesday

After discovering an empty tomb, the women were told by the angels to tell Christ's disciples He had risen. Peter and others ran back to the sepulchre to see for themselves. *Mark 16:4–8:* "And when they looked, they saw that the stone was rolled away: for it was very great.

"And entering into the sepulchre, they saw a young man sitting on the right side, clothed in a long white garment; and they were affrighted.

"And he saith unto them, Be not affrighted: Ye seek Jesus of Nazareth, which was crucified: he is risen; he is not here: behold the place where they laid him.

"But go your way, tell his disciples and Peter that he goeth before you into Galilee: there shall ye see him, as he said unto you.

"And they went out quickly, and fled from the sepulchre; for they trembled and were amazed: neither said they any thing to any man; for they were afraid."

Luke 24:10: "It was Mary Magdalene, and Joanna, and Mary the mother of James, and other women that were with them, which told these things unto the apostles.

"And their words seemed to them as idle tales, and they believed them not.

"Then arose Peter, and ran unto the sepulchre; and stooping down, he beheld the linen clothes laid by themselves, and departed, wondering in himself at that which was come to pass."

John 20:3–10: "Peter therefore went forth, and that other disciple, and came to the sepulchre.

"So they ran both together: and the other disciple did outrun Peter, and came first to the sepulchre.

"And he stooping down, and looking in, saw the linen clothes lying; yet went he not in.

"Then cometh Simon Peter following him, and went into the sepulchre, and seeth the linen clothes lie,

"And the napkin, that was about his head, not lying with the linen clothes, but wrapped together in a place by itself.

"Then went in also that other disciple, which came first to the sepulchre, and he saw, and believed.

"For as yet they knew not the scripture, that he must rise again from the dead.

"Then the disciples went away again unto their own home."

Thursday

Mary Magdalene remained at the sepulchre, and Jesus appeared to her.

John 20:11–17: "But Mary stood without at the sepulchre weeping: and as she wept, she stooped down, and looked into the sepulchre,

"And seeth two angels in white sitting, the one at the head, and the other at the feet, where the body of Jesus had lain.

"And they say unto her, Woman, why weepest thou? She saith unto them, Because they have taken away my Lord, and I know not where they have laid him.

"And when she had thus said, she turned herself back, and saw Jesus standing, and knew not that it was Jesus.

"Jesus saith unto her, Woman, why weepest thou? whom seekest thou? She, supposing him to be the gardener, saith unto him, Sir, if thou have borne him hence, tell me where thou hast laid him, and I will take him away.

"Jesus saith unto her, Mary. She turned herself, and saith unto him, Rabboni; which is to say, Master.

"Jesus saith unto her, Touch me not; for I am not yet ascended to my Father: but go to my brethren, and say unto them, I ascend unto my Father, and your Father; and to my God, and your God."

Mark 16:9–11. "Now when Jesus was risen early the first day of the week, he appeared first to Mary Magdalene, out of whom he had cast seven devils.

"And she went and told them that had been with him, as they mourned and wept.

"And they, when they had heard that he was alive, and had been seen of her, believed not."

Friday

Jesus appeared various other times to His disciples.

Mark 16:12–15: "After that he appeared in another form unto two of them, as they walked, and went into the country.

"And they went and told it unto the residue: neither believed they them.

"Afterward he appeared unto the eleven as they sat at meat, and upbraided them with their unbelief and hardness of heart, because they believed not them which had seen him after he was risen.

"And he said unto them, Go ye into all the world, and preach the gospel to every creature."

John 20:19–21: "Then the same day at evening, being the first day of the week, when the doors were shut where the disciples were assembled for fear of the Jews, came Jesus and stood in the midst, and saith unto them, Peace be unto you.

"And when he had so said, he shewed unto them his hands and his side. Then were the disciples glad, when they saw the Lord.

"Then said Jesus to them again, Peace be unto you: as my Father hath sent me, even so send I you."

Luke 24:13–16, 25–26, 28–31: "And, behold, two of them went that same day to a village called Emmaus, which was from Jerusalem about threescore furlongs.

"And they talked together of all these things which had happened.

"And it came to pass, that, while they communed together and reasoned, Jesus himself drew near, and went with them.

"But their eyes were holden that they should not know him:

"Then he said unto them, O fools, and slow of heart to believe all that the prophets have spoken:

"Ought not Christ to have suffered these things, and to enter into his glory?

"And they drew nigh unto the village, whither they went: and he made as though he would have gone further.

"But they constrained him, saying, Abide with us: for it is toward evening, and the day is far spent. And he went in to tarry with them.

"And it came to pass, as he sat at meat with them, he took bread, and blessed it, and brake, and gave to them.

"And their eyes were opened, and they knew him; and he vanished out of their sight."

John 20:24–31: "But Thomas, one of the twelve, called Didymus, was not with them when Jesus came.

"The other disciples therefore said unto him, We have seen the Lord. But he said unto them, Except I shall see in his hands the print of the nails, and put my finger into the print of the nails, and thrust my hand into his side, I will not believe.

"And after eight days again his disciples were within, and Thomas with them: then came Jesus, the doors being shut, and stood in the midst, and said, Peace be unto you.

"Then saith he to Thomas, Reach hither thy finger, and behold my hands; and reach hither thy hand, and thrust it into my side: and be not faithless, but believing.

"And Thomas answered and said unto him, My Lord and my God.

"Jesus saith unto him, Thomas, because thou hast seen me, thou hast believed: blessed are they that have not seen, and yet have believed.

"And many other signs truly did Jesus in the presence of his disciples, which are not written in this book:

"But these are written, that ye might believe that Jesus is the Christ, the Son of God; and that believing ye might have life through his name."

Saturday

We learn in the Book of Mormon that the entire world suffered great destruction and darkness for three days when Jesus Christ was crucified.

3 Nephi 8:20–23: "And it came to pass that there was thick darkness upon all the face of the land, insomuch that the inhabitants thereof who had not fallen could feel the vapor of darkness;

"And there could be no light, because of the darkness, neither candles, neither torches; neither could there be fire kindled with their fine and exceedingly dry wood, so that there could not be any light at all;

"And there was not any light seen, neither fire, nor glimmer, neither the sun, nor the moon, nor the stars, for so great were the mists of darkness which were upon the face of the land.

"And it came to pass that it did last for the space of three days that there was no light seen; and there was great mourning and howling and weeping among all the people continually; yea, great were the groanings of the people, because of the darkness and the great destruction which had come upon them."

Sunday

Through the darkness and destruction, the Nephites heard the voice of Jesus Christ. And after His Ascension back to God, Jesus appeared to the Nephites.

3 Nephi 9:13–16: "O all ye that are spared because ye were more righteous than they, will ye not now return unto me, and repent of your sins, and be converted, that I may heal you?

"Yea, verily I say unto you, if ye will come unto me ye shall have eternal life. Behold, mine arm of mercy is extended towards you, and whosoever will come, him will I receive; and blessed are those who come unto me.

"Behold, I am Jesus Christ the Son of God. I created the heavens and the earth, and all things that in them are. I was with the Father from the beginning. I am in the Father, and the Father in me; and in me hath the Father glorified his name.

"I came unto my own, and my own received me not. And the scriptures concerning my coming are fulfilled."

3 Nephi 10:18–19: "And it came to pass that in the ending of the thirty and fourth year, behold, I will show unto you that the people of Nephi who were spared, and also those who had been called Lamanites, who had been spared, did have great favors shown unto them, and great blessings poured out upon their heads, insomuch that soon after the ascension of Christ into heaven he did truly manifest himself unto them—

"Showing his body unto them, and ministering unto them; and an account of his ministry shall be given hereafter. Therefore for this time I make an end of my sayings."

3 Nephi 11:7–15: "Behold my Beloved Son, in whom I am well pleased, in whom I have glorified my name—hear ye him.

"And it came to pass, as they understood they cast their eyes up again towards heaven; and behold, they saw a Man descending out of heaven; and he was clothed in a white robe; and he came down and stood in the midst of them; and the eyes of the whole multitude were turned upon him, and they durst not open their mouths, even one to another, and wist not what it meant, for they thought it was an angel that had appeared unto them.

"And it came to pass that he stretched forth his hand and spake unto the people, saying:

"Behold, I am Jesus Christ, whom the prophets testified shall come into the world.

"And behold, I am the light and the life of the world; and I have drunk out of that bitter cup which the Father hath given me, and have glorified the Father in taking upon me the sins of the world, in the which I have suffered the will of the Father in all things from the beginning.

"And it came to pass that when Jesus had spoken these words the whole multitude fell to the earth; for they remembered that it had been prophesied among them that Christ should show himself unto them after his ascension into heaven.

"And it came to pass that the Lord spake unto them saying:

"Arise and come forth unto me, that ye may thrust your hands into my side, and also that ye may feel the prints of the nails in my hands and in my feet, that ye may know that I am the God of Israel, and the God of the whole earth, and have been slain for the sins of the world.

"And it came to pass that the multitude went forth, and thrust their hands into his side, and did feel the prints of the nails in his hands and in his feet; and this they did do, going forth one by one until they had all gone forth, and did see with their eyes and did feel with their hands, and did know of a surety and did bear record, that it was he, of whom it was written by the prophets, that should come."

Quote

"Our Lord has written the promise of resurrection, not in books alone, but in every leaf in springtime."

—Martin Luther (sixteenth-century Catholic priest)

Thoughtful Questions

- Many did not believe they saw a resurrected Jesus Christ. What do you think your thoughts would have been if you had seen Him?
- If you only heard the story of someone else who saw Him, would you still believe?
- Why could Mary not touch Jesus but the Nephites could?

Supporting Conference Address

D. Todd Christofferson, "The Resurrection of Jesus Christ," *Ensign*, May 2014.

Supporting Videos

"Jesus Is Laid in a Tomb," "He Is Risen: John the Beloved's Witness of the Resurrection," and "Chapter 43: Jesus Christ Appears to the Nephites"; available at lds.org/media-library.

Nation and Independence Day: Week 49

Daily Scripture Discussions

Monday

The highest power is God's power.

Romans 13:1: "Let every soul be subject unto the higher powers. For there is no power but of God: the powers that be are ordained of God."

Tuesday

Though government is instituted of God, we are ultimately responsible for a successful government.

D&C 134:1: "We believe that governments were instituted of God for the benefit of man; and that he holds men accountable for their acts in relation to them, both in making laws and administering them, for the good and safety of society."

Wednesday

Good citizens have good morals and values and seek to serve.

Romans 12:17–21: "Recompense to no man evil for evil. Provide things honest in the sight of all men.

"If it be possible, as much as lieth in you, live peaceably with all men.

"Dearly beloved, avenge not yourselves, but rather give place unto wrath: for it is written, Vengeance is mine; I will repay, saith the Lord.

"Therefore if thine enemy hunger, feed him; if he thirst, give him drink: for in so doing thou shalt heap coals of fire on his head.

"Be not overcome of evil, but overcome evil with good."

Thursday

Whether rich or poor, everyone has rights and deserves justice.

Psalm 82:3: "Defend the poor and fatherless: do justice to the afflicted and needy."

D&C 18:10: "Remember the worth of souls is great in the sight of God."

Friday

Laws are necessary for peace, and it's important for us to righteously uphold the law.

D&C 134:2: "We believe that no government can exist in peace, except such laws are framed and held inviolate as will secure to each individual the free exercise of conscience, the right and control of property, and the protection of life."

1 Peter 2:13–16: "Submit yourselves to every ordinance of man for the Lord's sake: whether it be to the king, as supreme;

"Or unto governors, as unto them that are sent by him for the punishment of evildoers, and for the praise of them that do well.

"For so is the will of God, that with well doing ye may put to silence the ignorance of foolish men:

"As free, and not using your liberty for a cloak of maliciousness, but as the servants of God."

Saturday

Choose to vote for good, honest people in elections.

D&C 98:10: "Wherefore, honest men and wise men should be sought for diligently, and good men and wise men ye should observe to uphold; otherwise whatsoever is less than these cometh of evil."

Mosiah 29:39: "Therefore, it came to pass that they assembled themselves together in bodies throughout the land, to cast in their voices concerning who should be their judges, to judge them according to the law which had been given them; and they were exceedingly rejoiced because of the liberty which had been granted unto them."

Sunday

King Mosiah taught his people about the challenges of both a righteous and unrighteous king and sought for a democracy.

Mosiah 29:31 38: "For behold I say unto you, the sins of many people have been caused by the iniquities of their kings; therefore their iniquities are answered upon the heads of their kings.

"And now I desire that this inequality should be no more in this land, especially among this my people; but I desire that this land be a land of liberty, and every man may enjoy his rights and privileges alike, so long as the Lord sees fit that we may live and inherit the land, yea, even as long as any of our posterity remains upon the face of the land.

"And many more things did king Mosiah write unto them, unfolding unto them all the trials and troubles of a righteous king, yea, all the travails of soul for their people, and also all the murmurings of the people to their king; and he explained it all unto them.

"And he told them that these things ought not to be; but that the burden should come upon all the people, that every man might bear his part.

"And he also unfolded unto them all the disadvantages they labored under, by having an unrighteous king to rule over them;

"Yea, all his iniquities and abominations, and all the wars, and contentions, and blood-shed, and the stealing, and the plundering, and the committing of whoredoms, and all manner of iniquities which cannot be enumerated—telling them that these things ought not to be, that they were expressly repugnant to the commandments of God.

"And now it came to pass, after king Mosiah had sent these things forth among the people they were convinced of the truth of his words.

"Therefore they relinquished their desires for a king, and became exceedingly anxious that every man should have an equal chance throughout all the land; yea, and every man expressed a willingness to answer for his own sins."

Quote

"Voting is the least arduous of a citizen's duties. He has the prior and harder duty of making up his mind."

—Ralph Barton Perry (philosopher)

Thoughtful Questions

- What do you love about our country?
- What can you do to be a good citizen?
- Why is it so important to participate in elections?
- Do you agree with King Mosiah?

Supporting Conference Address

Gordon B. Hinckley, "War and Peace," *Ensign*, May 2003.

Fear and Halloween: Week 50

Daily Scripture Discussions

Monday
Fear does not come from God.

2 Timothy 1:7: "For God hath not given us the spirit of fear; but of power, and of love, and of a sound mind."

Tuesday
Perfect love casts out fear.

1 John 4:18: "There is no fear in love; but perfect love casteth out fear: because fear hath torment. He that feareth is not made perfect in love."

Wednesday
Fear not, for the Lord is with you!

Psalm 118:6: "The Lord is on my side; I will not fear: what can man do unto me?"

Thursday
Keep the commandments, and don't fear the shame or hate of man.

2 Nephi 8:7: "Hearken unto me, ye that know righteousness, the people in whose heart I have written my law, fear ye not the reproach of men, neither be ye afraid of their revilings."

Isaiah 51:7: "Hearken unto me, ye that know righteousness, the people in whose heart is my law; fear ye not the reproach of men, neither be ye afraid of their revilings."

Friday
Don't worry about what others think; rely on the Lord for strength.

D&C 30:1: "Behold, I say unto you, David, that you have feared man and have not relied on me for strength as you ought."

Saturday

If you are prepared, you need not fear.

D&C 38:30: "I tell you these things because of your prayers; wherefore, treasure up wisdom in your bosoms, lest the wickedness of men reveal these things unto you by their wickedness, in a manner which shall speak in your ears with a voice louder than that which shall shake the earth; but if ye are prepared ye shall not fear."

Sunday

Faith cannot exist when you fear.

Matthew 8:26: "And he saith unto them, Why are ye fearful, O ye of little faith? Then he arose, and rebuked the winds and the sea; and there was a great calm."

Quote

"I think fearless is having fears but jumping anyway."

—Taylor Swift (singer)

Thoughtful Questions

- When do you feel afraid?
- How can you have faith instead of fear?
- Why would being prepared keep you from feeling fear?

Supporting Conference Address

Virginia H. Pearce, "Fear," *Ensign*, November 1992.

Gratitude and Thanksgiving: Week 51

Daily Scripture Discussions

Monday

Give thanks to the Lord through prayer.

Psalm 136:1: "O give thanks unto the Lord; for he is good: for his mercy endureth for ever."

Psalm 50:14: "Offer unto God thanksgiving; and pay thy vows unto the most High."

1 Chronicles 16:8: "Give thanks unto the Lord, call upon his name, make known his deeds among the people."

Tuesday

Remember to give thanks daily.

Alma 34:38: "That ye contend no more against the Holy Ghost, but that ye receive it, and take upon you the name of Christ; that ye humble yourselves even to the dust, and worship God, in whatsoever place ye may be in, in spirit and in truth; and that ye live in thanksgiving daily, for the many mercies and blessings which he doth bestow upon you."

Wednesday

Some like to praise the Lord in song and music.

Psalm 147:7: "Sing unto the Lord with thanksgiving; sing praise upon the harp unto our God."

D&C 136:28: "If thou art merry, praise the Lord with singing, with music, with dancing, and with a prayer of praise and thanksgiving."

Thursday

When we have a thankful heart, we are blessed.

D&C 78:19: "And he who receiveth all things with thankfulness shall be made glorious; and the things of this earth shall be added unto him, even an hundred fold, yea, more."

Friday

With a thankful heart, we can also call upon the Lord for our needs.

Philippians 4:6–7: "Be careful for nothing; but in every thing by prayer and supplication with thanksgiving let your requests be made known unto God.

"And the peace of God, which passeth all understanding, shall keep your hearts and minds through Christ Jesus."

Saturday

Daniel prayed and gave thanks even when it was outlawed.

Daniel 6:10: "Now when Daniel knew that the writing was signed, he went into his house; and his windows being open in his chamber toward Jerusalem, he kneeled upon his knees three times a day, and prayed, and gave thanks before his God, as he did aforetime."

Sunday

Only one of ten lepers came back to thank Jesus Christ.

Luke 17:12–19: "And as he entered into a certain village, there met him ten men that were lepers, which stood afar off:

"And they lifted up their voices, and said, Jesus, Master, have mercy on us.

"And when he saw them, he said unto them, Go shew yourselves unto the priests. And it came to pass, that, as they went, they were cleansed.

"And one of them, when he saw that he was healed, turned back, and with a loud voice glorified God,

"And fell down on his face at his feet, giving him thanks: and he was a Samaritan.

"And Jesus answering said, Were there not ten cleansed? but where are the nine?

"There are not found that returned to give glory to God, save this stranger.

"And he said unto him, Arise, go thy way: thy faith hath made thee whole."

Quote

"I don't have to chase extraordinary moments to find happiness—it's right in front of me if I'm paying attention and practicing gratitude."

—Brene Brown (author and speaker)

Thoughtful Questions

- What are you most grateful for in life?
- What little things are you grateful for?
- Have you taken the time lately to thank the Lord?
- What are other ways you can practice gratitude?

Supporting Conference Address

Thomas S. Monson, "The Divine Gift of Gratitude," *Ensign*, November 2010.

The Nativity and Christmas: Week 52

Daily Scripture Discussions

Monday

The Nativity story began with the Virgin Mary, who became the mother of Jesus.

Luke 1:26–35, 38: "And in the sixth month the angel Gabriel was sent from God unto a city of Galilee, named Nazareth,

"To a virgin espoused to a man whose name was Joseph, of the house of David; and the virgin's name was Mary.

"And the angel came in unto her, and said, Hail, thou that art highly favoured, the Lord is with thee: blessed art thou among women.

"And when she saw him, she was troubled at his saying, and cast in her mind what manner of salutation this should be.

"And the angel said unto her, Fear not, Mary: for thou hast found favour with God.

"And, behold, thou shalt conceive in thy womb, and bring forth a son, and shalt call his name Jesus.

"He shall be great, and shall be called the Son of the Highest: and the Lord God shall give unto him the throne of his father David:

"And he shall reign over the house of Jacob for ever; and of his kingdom there shall be no end.

"Then said Mary unto the angel, How shall this be, seeing I know not a man?

"And the angel answered and said unto her, The Holy Ghost shall come upon thee, and the power of the Highest shall overshadow thee: therefore also that holy thing which shall be born of thee shall be called the Son of God.

"And Mary said, Behold the handmaid of the Lord; be it unto me according to thy word. And the angel departed from her."

Tuesday

Mary was engaged to Joseph, who soon became the earthly father of Jesus.

Matthew 1:18–25: "Now the birth of Jesus Christ was on this wise: When as his mother Mary was espoused to Joseph, before they came together, she was found with child of the Holy Ghost.

"Then Joseph her husband, being a just man, and not willing to make her a publick example, was minded to put her away privily.

"But while he thought on these things, behold, the angel of the Lord appeared unto him in a dream, saying, Joseph, thou son of David, fear not to take unto thee Mary thy wife: for that which is conceived in her is of the Holy Ghost.

"And she shall bring forth a son, and thou shalt call his name Jesus: for he shall save his people from their sins.

"Now all this was done, that it might be fulfilled which was spoken of the Lord by the prophet, saying,

"Behold, a virgin shall be with child, and shall bring forth a son, and they shall call his name Emmanuel, which being interpreted is, God with us.

"Then Joseph being raised from sleep did as the angel of the Lord had bidden him, and took unto him his wife:

"And knew her not till she had brought forth her firstborn son: and he called his name Jesus."

Wednesday

While Mary was nine months pregnant, she and Joseph had to travel to Bethlehem. Unable to find any room in the Inn, Mary gave birth to Jesus Christ in a manger.

Luke 2:1–7: "And it came to pass in those days, that there went out a decree from Cæsar Augustus, that all the world should be taxed.

"(And this taxing was first made when Cyrenius was governor of Syria.)

"And all went to be taxed, every one into his own city.

"And Joseph also went up from Galilee, out of the city of Nazareth, into Judæa, unto the city of David, which is called Bethlehem; (because he was of the house and lineage of David:)

"To be taxed with Mary his espoused wife, being great with child.

"And so it was, that, while they were there, the days were accomplished that she should be delivered.

"And she brought forth her firstborn son, and wrapped him in swaddling clothes, and laid him in a manger; because there was no room for them in the inn."

Thursday

A multitude of angels appeared to shepherds watching over their field and told them Christ had been born. The shepherds eagerly went to visit Mary, Joseph, and the baby Jesus.

Luke 2:8–20: "And there were in the same country shepherds abiding in the field, keeping watch over their flock by night.

"And, lo, the angel of the Lord came upon them, and the glory of the Lord shone round about them: and they were sore afraid.

"And the angel said unto them, Fear not: for, behold, I bring you good tidings of great joy, which shall be to all people.

"For unto you is born this day in the city of David a Saviour, which is Christ the Lord.

"And this shall be a sign unto you; Ye shall find the babe wrapped in swaddling clothes, lying in a manger.

"And suddenly there was with the angel a multitude of the heavenly host praising God, and saying,

"Glory to God in the highest, and on earth peace, good will toward men.

"And it came to pass, as the angels were gone away from them into heaven, the shepherds said one to another, Let us now go even unto Bethlehem, and see this thing which is come to pass, which the Lord hath made known unto us.

"And they came with haste, and found Mary, and Joseph, and the babe lying in a manger.

"And when they had seen it, they made known abroad the saying which was told them concerning this child.

"And all they that heard it wondered at those things which were told them by the shepherds.

"But Mary kept all these things, and pondered them in her heart.

"And the shepherds returned, glorifying and praising God for all the things that they had heard and seen, as it was told unto them."

Friday

Wise men followed the star and brought gifts to Jesus. The wise men unintentionally alerted King Herod of this new "King of the Jews."

Matthew 2:1–2, 7–12: "Now when Jesus was born in Bethlehem of Judæa in the days of Herod the king, behold, there came wise men from the east to Jerusalem,

"Saying, Where is he that is born King of the Jews? for we have seen his star in the east, and are come to worship him.

"Then Herod, when he had privily called the wise men, inquired of them diligently what time the star appeared.

"And he sent them to Bethlehem, and said, Go and search diligently for the young child; and when ye have found him, bring me word again, that I may come and worship him also.

"When they had heard the king, they departed; and, lo, the star, which they saw in the east, went before them, till it came and stood over where the young child was.

"When they saw the star, they rejoiced with exceeding great joy.

"And when they were come into the house, they saw the young child with Mary his mother, and fell down, and worshipped him: and when they had opened their treasures, they presented unto him gifts; gold, and frankincense, and myrrh.

"And being warned of God in a dream that they should not return to Herod, they departed into their own country another way."

Saturday

The Christmas star and light are prominent symbols of Christmas. The Messiah brought light to a darkened world.

Isaiah 7:14: "Therefore the Lord himself shall give you a sign; Behold, a virgin shall conceive, and bear a son, and shall call his name Immanuel."

Matthew 2:9–10: "When they had heard the king, they departed; and, lo, the star, which they saw in the east, went before them, till it came and stood over where the young child was.

"When they saw the star, they rejoiced with exceeding great joy."

D&C 93:9: "The light and the Redeemer of the world; the Spirit of truth, who came into the world, because the world was made by him, and in him was the life of men and the light of men."

John 8:12: "Then spake Jesus again unto them, saying, I am the light of the world: he that followeth me shall not walk in darkness, but shall have the light of life."

Sunday

Gifts are a big part of our traditional Christmas. These gifts can remind us of the biggest gift we have been given: eternal life through our Savior Jesus Christ.

John 3:16: "For God so loved the world, that he gave his only begotten Son, that whosoever believeth in him should not perish, but have everlasting life."

Romans 6:23: "For the wages of sin is death; but the gift of God is eternal life through Jesus Christ our Lord."

Quote

"I will honor Christmas in my heart, and try to keep it all the year."

—Charles Dickens (author)

Thoughtful Questions

- What is your favorite part of the Nativity story?
- Do you think it was important that Jesus was born in a manger?
- What can we do to remember Jesus Christ and celebrate Him all year long?

Supporting Conference Address

Thomas S. Monson, "Christmas Is Love," First Presidency Christmas Devotional, December 2012.

Supporting Videos

"The Nativity" and "Good Tidings of Great Joy: The Birth of Jesus Christ," available at lds.org/bible-videos.

References

- The Book of Mormon
- The Holy Bible
- The Doctrine and Covenants
- The Pearl of Great Price
- The Guide to the Scriptures
- *True to the Faith: A Gospel Reference* (Salt Lake City: The Church of Jesus Christ of Latter-day Saints, 2004)
- www.lds.org
- www.youtube.com/MormonMessages

Bonus Content

I really hope this book makes a big difference for you and helps strengthen your family. As an added bonus, I'd love to offer you two extra weeks (chapters) and a complimentary video series with ideas on how to use this book to support families of all ages, write great church talks, plan engaging family home evenings, and more! Visit www.FortifyYourFamily.com/bookbonus to access your bonus content.

SCAN to visit

About the Author

Nicole Carpenter is an advocate of strong families. She believes in focusing first on strengthening mothers so they can fortify their children. Nicole is a mentor, speaker, and founder of *MOMentity.com*, a blog and online community for mothers, reaching out to moms in over seven different countries. She is also the creator of the Define Your Time time-management eCourse and the Mothers of Magnitude Academy. Nicole's parenting column publishes regularly on ksl.com and has been syndicated in several other online news sources.

Nicole graduated with a BA in public relations from Weber State University, where she also met her husband, Marty. They currently reside in Syracuse, Utah, and are raising four incredible children, including a set of identical twins. And to make it all happen, she may or may not rely on the Diet Dr Pepper and chocolate-covered toffee hidden in the fridge.